YOUNG MEN

OF

THE CROSS

By

Ed Erny

Published by One Mission Society
P. O. Box A, Greenwood, IN 46142

Pictured on front cover, L to R:
Crusaders: Hiles, Orkney, Poe, Miller, Stanley, Williamson, Haines, Oney, Thiele (Woods, not pictured)

One Mission Society
Box A, Greenwood, IN 46142

ISBN-13: 978-1-880338-13-1

Ed Erny
Young Men of the Cross

Printed in the United States of America
by Evangel Press, Nappanee, Indiana

CONTENTS

FOREWORD

We live in an age of short-term missions. I myself am forever indebted to this concept which in my youth was still something of an innovation. In the early 1950s—and following the world's worst war which bereft our planet of millions of lives—revival had come again to the United States. A young evangelist named Billy Graham was God's instrument, and he was filling America's coliseums, drawing thousands of hearers. Concurrent with this phenomenon came the birth of a plethora of new evangelical endeavors, all targeting mid-century youth intent on winning the world to Jesus Christ. Youth for Christ, Campus Crusade for Christ, Inter-Varsity Fellowship, Operation Mobilization, and Youth with a Mission were all born.

At a time when the Western world still viewed the term "crusade" as heroic and noble with little concern for the stigma that offends the Moslem populations in Asia and Africa, Billy Graham had labeled his great meetings evangelistic crusades. At about the same time OMS, a little-known mission, determined to repeat an epochal campaign launched by her founders, Charles Cowman and E.A. Kilbourne. Their goal was to place the Scriptures and plan of salvation in every home in a nation, something never before attempted. It was initially called The Great Village Campaign but later the Every Creature Crusade. It was begun in 1913. In 1916 Cowman, who had close ties with God's Bible School in Cincinnati, felt inspired to challenge GBS boys to join in the monumental effort. Ten volunteered and, along with their Japanese teammates, they would walk thousands of miles in remote mountains and inhospitable terrain, seeking out every one of Japan's 10,400,000 homes.

This truly heroic and difficult venture was completed in 1918. The lives and destinies of every one of those evangelists, later labeled crusaders, were forever enriched and permanently altered.

My passion to write this record is inspired by the fact that in 1958, following a great outpouring of the Holy Spirit on the campus of Asbury College, God all but drove me to postpone my wedding for two years to join the second Every Creature Crusade. Most of our generation of crusaders again sailed for Japan, a nation still recovering from the horrors of World War II. Mission leaders, however, had just determined to inaugurate the ECC in Taiwan and requested my services. I hardly knew where this island, then called Formosa, was. I would soon make intimate acquaintance with Formosa. In so doing my life, like that of the early crusaders, would be forever changed. But that story we have reserved for another book soon to follow.

Ed Erny
Greenwood, Indiana

Chapter 1

BEGINNINGS

The audacious plan to reach every home in Japan with the Gospel of Jesus Christ began in 1910 with two former telegraphers. Despite their executive gifts, neither Charles Cowman nor Ernest Kilbourne had more than a high school education. Had they the benefit of a university diploma or string of degrees after their names, the quixotic notion of literally taking the Gospel to every creature would likely have never been attempted.

In the late 1800s, Charles Cowman and Ernest Kilbourne were living in Chicago. They were employed in the large Western Union office where they had achieved executive status. Both men were full of ambition and common sense. They were also practical enough to know that impetuous and foolhardy religious notions have no place in the hurly-burly business life of that great city.

The fly in the ointment was Charles Cowman's wife, Lettie. She was the daughter of a banker in Iowa, and great plans for an education in fine arts in Europe had been made. But those plans were confounded by her friendship with Charles Cowman, a young telegrapher with a farm upbringing. To her parents' dismay, Charles and Lettie married. Charles took a position in a telegraph office in Colorado and later was transferred to Chicago where he proceeded to climb the ladder in the prestigious Western Union company.

Her early upbringing inspired in Lettie a love for opera. It was this passion alone that enticed her to attend a service at a local Methodist church which that night featured a noted opera star. What Letttie did not know was that this gifted soprano had "gotten religion." That fact became immediately obvious when she began to recite the tragic and glorious tale of her conversion—how all the fame and glamour of opera left her jaded, a lost soul futilely seeking to fill an empty heart. She discovered that all the renown and trinkets of the world could not assuage the terrible inner hunger. Now with a heart overflowing with the fervor of her newfound faith, she sang for His glory alone. In the opera star's quest for meaning in the world's glitter, Lettie saw the chronicle of her own empty life.

At the invitation, a formerly distasteful "altar call," Lettie stumbled to the front to kneel among a small sea of children. (The service, it seems, had actually been billed as a children's service.) There it was that Lettie knelt, wept, confessed her sin and opened her heart to Jesus as Savior.

Charles loved Lettie deeply and the report of her conversion moved him. Yet he told himself that, given the demands of the rough Chicago business world, religion was an inconvenient commodity.

The one thing, however, Charles could never do was deny his wife anything. So, when she lovingly, persistently and indefatigably insisted that Charles accompany her to a revival at the Grace Methodist Church where she was now attending, he had no choice but to comply.

The evangelist was eloquent, passionate, but Charles was a practical man and, though soft spoken, uncommonly strong willed. He had withstood other powerful altar calls before. When the response was not all that the evangelist had hoped for, he resorted to a device he had doubtless used before and found most persuasive.

The saved and happy souls bound for heaven he invited to join him at the front of the church. As for the others, they could remain in their seats, "in the wilderness, on the other side of Jordan."

As Charles glumly watched his beloved leave him and make her way to the front, he became convinced that what he was seeing was the terrible enactment of his eternal destiny, the great gulf of which Christ spoke in the story of the rich man and Lazarus.

Nevertheless, Charles did not respond. Still, he knew the foundations of the huge castle of his pride were crumbling. After the benediction, Charles could not wait to get home, a quiet place where he could collapse in abject surrender at the feet of Jesus. When they arrived at the front door, Charles entered swiftly and, without turning on the lights, fell sobbing beside the sofa with Lettie beside him. It was a decision from which he would never look back.

Charles Cowman never did things by halves. Now that he was a Christian, it was incumbent upon him to follow Christ all the way and confront all he met with the good news and incredible joy that was his.

The next day at the Western Union office, he accosted his friend and colleague, Ernest Kilbourne. Charles had never taken a course in soul-winning, nor did he know much about scripture and theology. This effort, in his eyes, was an utter failure. He trudged grimly home, convinced that he had made a fool of himself and embarrassed the sweet name of Jesus.

No one on the planet could have been more surprised than Charles when he entered the office the next morning to find Kilbourne shuffling uneasily and on the verge of tears. "Sit down, Charles." He spoke gently but with an awful sincerity. "I've been thinking about what you said yesterday. I didn't sleep all night. Dear friend, will you please pray with me. Tell me how to receive Jesus as my Savior." The two men knelt. A union was formed that day that would endure through eternity, to God's glory and the salvation of innumerable souls.

In tandem, the two men set about to lead every telegrapher possible to Christ. Within six months, more than 50 of their colleagues had placed their faith in Christ. They organized a fellowship which they named the "Telegraphers' Band." This organization would eventually have chapters in many major telegraph offices, both in the U.S. and overseas. But this was only a start. Cowman next opened a mission for derelicts in the Chicago slums. At the same time, he also enrolled in night classes at Moody Bible Institute.

Chapter 2

THE MAN FROM JAPAN

A fellow student at MBI, who also attended Grace Methodist Church, was a foreigner named Juji Nakada. He would one day be ranked among Japan's three greatest preachers. In Japan, Juji had been educated in a seminary which had lamentably been influenced by so-called higher criticism. He married and took a pastorate on the wind-swept, rock-strewn Kurile Islands. The landscape of those remote, sparsely-populated islands seemed to in every way mirror Nakada's own spirit. On the verge of resigning his pastorate, he was sent a magazine that told of American evangelist, D.L. Moody, whose great power he attributed to being "filled with the Holy Spirit." Greatly moved, Nakada told his wife that he must go to America to Moody's school to get filled with the Holy Spirit. It was either that or leave the ministry. Nakada's wife immediately offered him her dowry jewels to pay for his fare.

Upon arrival, Juji enrolled in Moody Bible Institute. One morning after a chapel message by an Indian evangelist, Reverend David, he stumbled to his room, fell across his bed, and cried for the empowerment of the Spirit of God. The experience left Nakada a new man in every way. He began attending the nearby Grace Methodist Church, and there it was he met Charles Cowman and Ernest Kilbourne, who had themselves recently been filled with the Spirit.

Under Nakada's influence, the vision of the men now became focused on distant fields, the world in which multiplied millions lived and died without ever hearing the name of Jesus. Juji, of course, was a fervent advocate for the needs of his own nation, Japan, which, after centuries of isolation, had recently been opened to Western nations, thanks to Admiral Perry's famed armada in 1852. The following generation of Japanese was shamelessly eager to imitate all things Western, even to inquire into the character of this new and powerful religion called Christianity.

In 1901, the Cowmans and Juji Nakada opened a Gospel hall in the downtown Jimbo-Cho district of Tokyo. Ernest Kilbourne, who refused to leave the homeland till every debt was discharged, arrived with his wife a year later. It is recorded that evangelistic meetings were held without remission for 3,000 consecutive nights. As the two Americans studied the difficult Japanese tongue, each evening they witnessed the eloquent power of their Japanese colleague, who preached with consistent and amazing fervor. Every night there were seekers at the altar. This glorious spectacle impressed upon Nakada's American colleagues and their wives a fact and principle which would become a foundation of their new mission. "Japan," Cowman wrote, "will never be won to Christ by foreigners. It must be done by her own sons and daughters." With hundreds and eventually thousands coming to Christ at the Jimbo-Cho hall, they were soon faced with another challenge: what now to do with this throng of new converts?

The answer, of course, must be the planting of Gospel centers (later to become churches) and, above all, a Bible school where young people could be trained to preach and evangelize. The result would be one of the great churches of Asia, the Japan Holiness Church. By 1930 this small band of zealots with Juji Nakada as bishop had become the third largest denomination in the country. How to account for this phenomenon? Cowman was often asked. The reply was that this was a vision, a method that God had given the men. Charles referred to it as "the pattern shown us on the mount." In a word it was simply that the foreign missionaries' primary responsibility was to serve as God's instruments in the training of nationals. These graduates, now imbued with a knowledge of God and Scripture and filled with the Holy Spirit, were to be the nation's evangelists, pastors and church founders. Thus, OMS was born and from it came the Japanese Holiness Church which would one day serve as a model for churches in Korea, China, India, Latin America and Europe.

Chapter 3

THE MACEDONIAN CALL

Early on, the OMS founders were troubled by the same thing that stirred the heart of Hudson Taylor and led to the founding of the China Inland Mission. Since the great Asian cities were mainly located in the coastal areas, this is where missionaries concentrated their efforts. The result was that the vast populations in the interior of Japan and China were virtually untouched by the Gospel. Most had never seen a missionary or pastor.

As early as 1903, there appeared in *Electric Messages*, the monthly magazine of the Cowman-Kilbourne mission, an ever increasing burden, referred to as their Macedonian call. This was an urge to evangelize Japan's interior regions. One of the first of these articles appeared in the December '04 issue of the magazine under the title "Echigo." Kilbourne wrote:

> Last summer there came into our Sunday morning English Bible class in Tokyo a high school teacher, 28 years of age, from a town called Echigo, 300 miles to the west. "In our town," he told me, "there are no Christians or churches anywhere near." This province, we learned, has a population of 1,800,000 souls. There are nearly 2,000 villages there, all lying in utter darkness.

Increasing concern for the remote areas continued to appear in *Electric Messages*. A 1904 issue reported "a few days ago came a letter from the homeland enclosing several dollars, designated for itinerant work in the neglected interior parts." Cowman said, "God seemed to whisper to us that the time had come to go to Echigo." After praying about it, they recruited a Gospel band of six who were to make a ten-day trip to "spy out the land," preach the Gospel, and distribute Scripture portions and tracts. "We hope then to determine the best location for a mission station," they said.

In the next issue of the magazine, Cowman reported that God seemed to be drawing his attention to another large interior province with a population of 860,000, likewise untouched by the Gospel. "But how are we going to find either the men or the money to carry the Gospel to these thousands upon thousands of villages around us?" he asked.

Robert Atchinson, an acquaintance from their God's Bible School days in Cincinnati, agreed to lead a vanguard of young Japanese evangelists in the first attempt to reach interior areas. In his testimony in *Electric Messages*, Atchinson repeated the challenge, "How am I going to carry the Gospel to the unreached towns and villages? I then remembered a bicycle that the Lord had given me in Cincinnati, but, alas, I couldn't ride it. I made up my mind to learn and I did in a hurry." Below the article is a photo showing Atchinson and his bicycle. Tied to the rack on the handlebars is a huge bundle of Gospel tracts. "My wife and I are up at 4 a.m.," he said, "and, after getting something to eat, we leave the house, arriving at a village in time to meet the farmers coming into market."

Later other associates from Cincinnati Bible school days also joined Cowman and Kilbourne in these preliminary efforts. Their names, and little else about them, appear in early issues of the mission magazine. They were Charles Clark, K.E. Aurell, Fred Briggs and brothers Heslip, Bruster and Lassen. Brother Voss later joined them. Sadly, he was only in the country three months before his untimely death at age 30.

Hence it should be stated that in 1903, at least ten years before the formal launching of The Great Village Campaign, OMS Gospel bands, consisting of Bible school students or recent graduates and led by young missionaries like Atchinson and Clark, were already targeting the interior with the Gospel. From these efforts came good fruit, including the opening of a number of Gospel halls.

The usual procedure at this time was to, upon entering a town for a Gospel campaign, rent a hall with accompanying rooms for lodging. Once settled, the first item on the agenda was the so-called "Gospel march." Team members advertised their presence with a parade down "main street" accompanied by a vociferous beating of drums. In the afternoon, the boys would again make their way through the heart of the village or town, announcing that good news would be proclaimed that night in the Gospel hall. Along the route, they distributed tracts and handbills to onlookers. These marches aroused considerable interest. Many in rural interior villages had never before seen a light-skinned foreigner. Their arrival would attract a following of local citizens, intent on discovering these curious creatures for themselves. Usually, from the first night on, attendance at the Gospel hall would be a hundred or more.

Services began with rousing music followed by a fervently proclaimed message resulting in seekers almost every evening. After about six weeks, new believers would be organized into a small group which would meet regularly in the Gospel hall and be pastored by one of the team members, chosen to stay behind while the others moved on to the next town or province. The testimonies of the new converts often appeared in the mission magazine. Even today, they make exciting reading.

In the September '09 issue of *Electric Messages*, was this report:

> Open air meetings in the parks are being greatly blessed. As one looks over the immense crowds numbering between 200 and 2,000, he sees people of all classes and occupations: professors, students, businessmen and coolies—both rich and poor. They stand together, as though lost to their surroundings and listening with hungry hearts to the gracious words of salvation and freedom for all. Many will stand for hours without seeming to tire. When the meetings are over, some still linger and come to inquire more of the way of salvation. Often young converts will rise and tell of their joy in salvation and exhort the people to get saved. It does our hearts good to see the converts

turning almost immediately after conversion to soul-winning.

Most who attended the Gospel services were men. Evangelist S. Mikame, however, wrote, "We have some women who are bringing forth fruit." Brother T. Watanabe reported, "The Lord gave me two theater actors who repented with tears and received Christ as Savior."

In the May issue of the magazine are reports from several villages:

> In Kaso we held two street meetings for crowds of earnest listeners, each one of whom received a Gospel portion. We believe these are hungry hearts that will be won for Jesus.
>
> In Gioda, another village, we held three open-air meetings besides the Gospel distribution. The crowds all listened earnestly.
>
> We also visited Irugwa, a good-size village, which has never heard the Gospel. We then walked to a place called Oume, giving out the Word to 14 villages on the way. We continued distributing till our tracts gave out. Pray for 14,000 darkened homes into which these printed Gospel message came that the light may spring up.

The October 1912 issue of the magazine reported:

> To the northwest of Tokyo in an area with a population of 150,000, a band of four of us came to a place where a large heathen festival was in progress. We encountered great crowds thronging the streets so we decided to hold an open-air service. On the 29th despite the rain, we visited 2,680 homes in Senju with the Word of life.
>
> One of our evangelists told of meeting a pathetic hermit. "At Makinogawa," he said, "I found a man who had been living at the foot of a hill in a little hut for ten years, ill and

> gradually dying. I told him of Christ and His salvation. Thank God, the light shone into his hungry heart. After I prayed for him, he prayed: 'Oh, God, there are many gods, all of whom have cast me out and could not save me, but you receive me and can save me'."

Where rented rooms were not available, the team lodged in hotels or inns. This provided fruitful opportunities to witness to the employees. A team member wrote:

> At the hotel where we were staying, we had the joy of seeing one of the maids accept salvation. The night before she came to our meeting, she said she was convinced that there was a true God. The next morning at breakfast she told us how hungry her heart was. With joy we repeated the Gospel story, after which she repented and was truly saved. What a shine she had on her face!

Another reported:

> One evening we could find no place to stay so we crossed over to an adjoining county and lodged in an inn at Tanahsi. Usually, in distribution, if none are at home, we leave a Gospel pamphlet under the door or in some other convenient place with a note of explanation. On occasion, the recipients respond with a letter of thanks to Cowman and Kilbourne whose names and address appear on the tract.
>
> One memorable letter came from a Miss Imai in excellent English. "Dear Sirs, Many thanks for your literature. At night on the third, after the family slept, I crept out of my bed and entered another room and there I prayed. I confessed all my sins and I am sure that God has forgiven them. I believe that Christ died on the cross that I might get rid of my sins. I know Jesus is constantly looking upon me so I feel that I cannot do or say anything that is wrong. If I continue to sin after I have asked God for forgiveness of

my past sins, I shall be more abominable than before I repented."

Another wrote: "Dear Sirs, I promised God that I would no longer do wrong. I am very glad that I was led to the knowledge of salvation while I am still young. And now I am longing to lead my family and friends to the way of salvation also. One of my intimate friends is willing to repent and to become a Christian with me so please also tell her the story of the Gospel. Miss Nihi Miai."

In the October 1913 issue, following the official launch of The Great Village Campaign, appears this report:

Brother Yoko Jina, having finished a distribution to about 38 villages, came rejoicing because he had seen 11 men and women either saved or declaring themselves seekers. At one place called Mihara, he found that almost all the inhabitants were deformed lepers. Four of them became seekers and gave us their names and addresses so we can send Christian literature to them.

All, however, were not as happy to receive the good news. At the close of the message one evening, the evangelist asked his listeners if they had understood what he had said. In the rear a man stood up to declare:

I do not understand what you have preached. I do not like Christianity! I heard you say that there is only one God in the universe. Do you mean Amaterasu Okama, our emperor, is not god? If you mean that he is not god, then your religion is against the constitution of Japan, and we cannot agree with your treachery and are opposed to your preaching.

Another in the audience, emboldened by this speech, cried:

> You Christians always talk of sin, sin, sin. It makes me disgusted. If one is going to always think that this is or that is sin, then there is no pleasure in life. The best way is to be unconcerned about sins. Otherwise one cannot enjoy himself.

One of the Gospel teams focused their efforts on Saitama Province, a campaign made possible by a generous gift of $3,000 from Dr. Blackstone, the author of the book and song entitled, *Jesus Is Coming Again.* Saitama had a population of 1,304,000 souls and boasted 5,777 shrines and temples with 1,818 priests. This amounts to one shrine for every 226 persons and a priest for every 717 souls. No resident missionaries or Christians workers were located in that province.

Here, in one of the early meetings, 13 accepted Christ. Others promised to return to talk further about the Christian faith. The next day they showed up at the hotel where the evangelists were staying and asked for Brother Aurell. "We do not quite understand why Christianity is so valuable," they said. It gave our brother so much joy to tell them. And in about 30 minutes they were quite willing to acknowledge that they were sinners and needed a Savior like Jesus. And before they left the room, they, too, had accepted Him and were rejoicing.

Chapter 4

THE GREAT VILLAGE CAMPAIGN

Now the mission began to draw up plans to systematically reach every village and prefecture (county), and thereafter entire provinces. Cowman and Kilbourne proceeded to devise a grand vision for accomplishing this goal, a goal which in the entire history of Christendom had never been attempted.

Thus in the latter part of 1913, The Great Village Campaign was officially launched. Lettie Cowman in her book *Missionary Warrior* tells of how this came about, and one cannot do better then to quote this passage.

> One evening a little company of our new missionaries met for language study. None was permitted to speak a word of English. A young missionary asked in broken Japanese, "Brother Cowman, have the villages of Japan been given an opportunity to hear the Gospel? If not, why not?" The words were like a flaming arrow flung into our hearts. The study class was changed into a prayer service. At ten o'clock Charles went to his room and at midnight was still at his desk. I urged him to retire but he said, "I cannot. The burden is too great." At dawn, he was still there. He greeted me with a cheery good morning and told me he had met the Lord in the night silence and that He had unfolded to him a plan whereby every person in Japan might hear the Gospel in the next five years.
>
> In his business-like manner, he had jotted down statistics and figures, the number of provinces in Japan, their populations, and the number of homes:

The population of Japan – 60,000,000
Number of homes – 10,400,000

Cost of scripture portions and expense of workers - $100,000

There followed the outline of a systematic campaign. Provinces were to be taken, one by one, with a force of workers committed to visiting every town, village and home. He calculated that two missionaries and ten Japanese could visit the homes of an entire province in six months' time. If the force could be doubled and tripled, several provinces could be undertaken. He was sure that 50 missionaries and 250 Japanese could complete the work in a year. However, among our number, only one or two missionaries could be spared for this particular work. The plan seemed audacious for those days but his faith and vision had grasped it as God-given, and he made no plans for retreating or turning aside. Nothing seemed left but to carry it out.

He said to one of his fellow missionaries, "We have just skirted the borders. Eighty percent of the people have never heard one word of the Gospel, even after 60 years of Christian effort. There is no need to wait for counsels, conferences and committees. To get at the work and do it, that's the thing. This is God's set time. We must act as if we are the only ones commissioned. We can wait no longer. Why in these days of colossal business schemes can we not undertake the King's business as something that requires haste and summon every loyal disciple?"

To friends at home, Charles wrote, "The Great Village Campaign has been launched and it is the subject of much comment throughout missionary circles." It was quickly noised about that The Oriental Missionary Society, a faith mission, with no guaranteed funds or influential home committees, a mission that would not go into debt, even if worse came to worse, had undertaken to place the Gospel in the 10,400,000 homes in Japan.

> After a thing has been done, everybody is ready to declare it easy, but, before it has been done, it is called impossible. Someone said, "What can Charles Cowman be thinking of?" The news created a thrill of surprise and wonder. We received letters of both encouragement and discouragement. To the latter he replied, "Faith will be staggered even by loose stones in the way if we look man-ward. If we look God-ward, faith will not be staggered even by mountains."

Years later, in retrospect, Charles' co-worker, E. A. Kilbourne wrote of this venture, commenting upon the prayer life of Charles Cowman:

> Again we hear Brother Cowman pleading and now the burden of his soul is The Great Village Campaign. To reach every creature in Japan was the desire of his heart. Impossible, the enemy insistently whispered. Just think of the millions of homes within this empire of 60,000,000 people; just think of the congested cities with their interminable alleys; just think of the great mountains everywhere to be crossed; just think of transporting the literature to the innumerable villages of the far interior; just think of the thousands of homes hidden in the vastness of snow-clad mountains; just think of the impassable roads and paths to be traveled; just think of the inhospitable reception one must meet among fanatical idolaters; just think of the lack of hotel accommodations in the country districts; just think of a hundred other difficulties that presented themselves to the pleading soul and how they were magnified into mountains.
>
> But Brother Cowman knew God as the author and fulfiller of His promises. Mountains must be cast into the sea; trees rooted up; every valley exalted and every hill made low before this man on his knees, and thus it was. He delighted in the Word. He took a special gratification in pleading the series of promises containing those remarkable, inimitable

words: "whosoever, anything, all things," and entered into the realm of impossibilities to seek God and be found of Him.

The first contribution to The Great Village Campaign came from Ernest Kilbourne. It was $5, all the money he possessed. "$5," Cowman said, "and faith in God." Now, for the first time in issues of *Electric Messages*, there appear maps of Japan almost entirely in black, outlining with dotted lines, the provinces and districts to be covered. The literature they chose to distribute consisted primarily of a scripture booklet entitled "Way of Peace." It explained God's plan of salvation drawn from the four Gospels and other scriptures. Once a prefecture or province had been covered, the area would then appear in white on the map of Japan in subsequent magazines. In time, the entire sea of black would be transformed into a glorious sea of white, indicating that the entire nation had been reached.

From month to month now appeared heartening words and the progressive field of white, showing that a certain prefecture or entire province had been completed, and "we are moving on to other provinces until the millions have been reached." And always in bold letters, **"We need your help to do it."**

In the OMS magazine, now renamed *The Missionary Standard*, Brother Aurell reported that at Awawta an old man had stubbornly refused to receive the glad tidings. "I felt so sorry for him because he did not know what he was rejecting. I felt led to ask, 'Dear friend, if you were to die tonight, are you prepared?' This unexpected question seemed to alarm him to such an extent that he immediately took off his cap and held out both hands to receive the booklet and tract. Then he gave due attention to all that was said on this momentous question. Pray that he may be saved."

Some who received the booklets were eager to know exactly what advantages would result from joining "this religion." "Will it help me financially?" one asked. "If I should want to borrow 100 yen ($5 U.S.), would Christians loan me the money?" Others asked, "If we become Christians, will we be healed of our bodily ailments?" Some inquired if joining Christianity would require them to work. In many homes, it was clear they supposed that by becoming a Christian they would enjoy prosperity, even profit from questionable enterprises. The gambler, the thief, the harlot and saloon keeper thought that worshipping the right god would result in certain prosperity and provide all manner of benefits. "Could Jesus," they inquired, "bring success to my business?" Some hoped that Christianity would result in mental acuity. An army officer asked, "Will I be able to better learn English?"

For Japanese, raised in Buddhism with its prime tenet of reincarnation, a great concern related to the benefits of the new religion in the afterlife. "If I become a Christian," they would ask, "will I be rich in the next reincarnation?" Most, however, did not suppose that being a Christian would result in any moral improvement.

In 1913, another young evangelist from the U.S. joined the work. We know very little about this young man who is simply referred to as Brother Ken. His team was assigned to Kikai Island. On arriving there, he reported, "I began an open-air meeting and about 200 people attended. Five were dealt with personally and sought the Lord. I spent just 60 days in the work and reached 34 villages and 20,000 souls. Altogether I have held 60 meetings and 30 men and women have made a profession of faith and a hundred more have become inquirers. I've passed out 90 Bibles and 30 other salvation books were sold. There were 9,000 persons who attended my meetings. Hallelujah!"

A photo in the March 14 issue of *The Missionary Standard* shows four missionary evangelists poring over a map charting the progress of the campaign. The young men are Brothers Aurell, Briggs, Lassen and Oney. Aurell is identified as the superintendent of the bands. Not pictured is Brother Clark who also headed one of the bands. In Aurell's article entitled "The Real Conditions in the Villages," he writes:

When we arrived, we took our dinner at the best (!) hotel. Having taken off our shoes, we were led to a furniture-less room, cold as an ice house! We sat down on little square cushions which the maid had placed on the floor for each of us. In a few moments, she brought a tin box with a few pieces of glowing charcoal; also, a dainty little teapot and hot water.

We learned that the maid who served us also provided sordid services to lustful men. She is a sort of indentured servant and cannot leave until she has earned enough money to redeem herself. We felt so sorry for her. I told her about the best friend one can have—Jesus. Some girls really do repent and accept Jesus, but for many circumstances make it almost impossible. They need our prayers.

Aurell goes on to describe the homes he visited in that village. He says, "We find that almost in every one of the 200 homes in the village there is continual controversy, squabbling between man and wife, as well as children."

Other sad stories: "My son has left and has forgotten us." "Our daughter has run away." "Father spends all his days lying on his hands and drinking." "My uncle deceived me." "We hate the priest. He is a lazy, useless man."

One of the consequences of traversing the rough, narrow paths and mountain trails was foot problems—sore, swollen feet, terrible blisters. Usually, almost every day, arduous treks were made over the stony trails carrying large bundles of Gospel literature. Almost all suffered, not only from sore feet but worn-out shoes or shoes in desperate need of repair. In these pre-Nike days, thin leather-soled shoes did not last long. American team members recall that on the average they wore out one pair of shoes per month.

When the team reached Chuaji Island, they commenced the evangelistic effort with the usual street marches, along the way inviting people to the rented Gospel hall that evening. About 900 came. One night Brother Shoya spoke on the wonderful power of God to transform the life of a sinner, making him a child of God. One of the seekers was a man whose face bore witness to a life of degradation. He confessed that he had once been a notorious gambler. He had also been an itinerant actor in a circus, traveling from town to town. Short of cash, he resorted to robbery. He was soon caught, arrested and imprisoned. After a few years, he was released but before long had returned to his old ways, only worse. In a botched robbery, he murdered five people. He was arrested and again incarcerated, this time in the notorious Matsupi Prison. Here he heard a sermon by an OMS evangelist, Brother Koji, himself a former thief and a murderer. Through his message, Soga was brought to Christ. When released, he began preaching the Gospel and helping to take God's Word to the interior villages of Awaji.

During the Awaji Island campaign, a team member, Brother Horive, met a Buddhist priest who curiously seemed overjoyed to meet him. He explained that "although I am a Buddhist priest, I realize that the real need of the world is Christianity." He said that he often called on pastors or missionaries and had gained helpful thoughts from them. This man is quite a writer and has authored several tracts in an effort to improve Buddhism. As Brother Horive prayed for this man, he reverently bowed his head. We feel he may be very near to the kingdom.

The great campaign was now fully underway and progressed from town to village to every home in a county or prefecture and then on to outlying islands (even distant Okinawa) and finally entire provinces. Cowman and Kilbourne at each step had to come to terms with the demands of this undertaking. More and more they understood the cost not only in dollars and yen but also in human muscle, flesh and blood.

Chapter 5

A VENTURE OF FAITH

Though a faith mission, modeled to a large degree after the work of George Mueller and Hudson Taylor, OMS did not adopt their rule that financial needs should be made known to God alone and not to man. Following the example of the Apostle Paul in II Corinthians, chapters eight and nine, they made bold and urgent appeals to give liberally to, as it were, "save the starving ones in Jerusalem."

The campaign, which was initiated with just $5, Kilbourne's gift, would cost a great sum for not only printing millions of Gospel tracts and booklets but also for paying the salaries and expenses of both missionaries and scores of native workers. In this period, faith missions seldom required that foreign missionaries take personal responsibility for raising their own support. Ostensibly all were challenged to share the burden and to "pray in the needed funds," but at the end of each month, payroll time or when bills came due, it was primarily Cowman and Kilbourne who faced the stark demand of outstanding bills and deficits in terms of dollars and yen. Every issue of the magazine *Electric Messages* unapologetically contained strong and urgent appeals for financial support.

For the missions' two American leaders, long experienced in the business world, familiarity with common-sense funding techniques stood them in good stead. In Asian nations of that time, where people subsisted on mere pennies a day, the cost of most commodities was a fraction of the price for the same goods and services in the U.S. This fact proved a powerful tool in appealing for funds. A dollar in Japan, Kilbourne pointed out, would finance the printing of huge numbers of tracts and Gospels and evangelize 1,000 homes. Was there any greater bargain or wiser investment on earth?

Ten villages could be reached for $20, an entire county for $300 and a province for $3,000. These powerful appeals fueled the great vision of literally walking for Christ to every home in the nation. (It was admitted, however, that there were doubtless some villages or homes that were impossible to find and did not appear on any maps.) Churches, Sunday school classes and Christian companies were urged "to reach an entire county or province with the Gospel."

A few wealthy Christian men also caught the vision. The hymn writer and philanthropist, Dr. Blackstone, was an admirer of Cowman and Kilbourne, and one who "attempted great things for God." He gave OMS gifts as large as $30,000 at a time to promote The Every Village Campaign.

OMS leaders never appealed for sacrifices greater than they themselves were prepared to make. They and their families learned to subsist on incredibly little. Lettie remembered the day they sat down with a visitor to little more than bread and water. Kilbourne owned but one suit. During the week, it was his habit to leave the suit coat open but on Sundays, to affect an appropriate reverence, it was buttoned.

For the small mission to Japan, far from friends in the U.S. and without either a homeland headquarters or mission representatives, the primary vehicle for enlisting support was the mission magazine. In each issue there were appeals printed in bold type or enclosed in large boxes so as not to be overlooked. In a single issue of the magazine, there were often as many as ten or more solicitations. These appeals were not only for The Great Village Campaign but also the support of the Bible school, national workers, revival campaigns, publishing of books and even the entertaining of visiting evangelists.

With no guarantee of support from wealthy individuals or homeland organizations, the Cowmans felt it incumbent upon themselves to spend several months each year visiting homeland churches and camp meetings. This, Charles and Lettie did for 15 consecutive years, traveling back and forth by steamship. These voyages are all recorded and dated on the flyleaf of Charles' Bible. Upon arrival in California, their itinerary kept them on the road almost without pause. The Cowman's correspondence speaks of "hundreds of trips" to churches, conventions and camp meetings. Everywhere Charles carried his maps of Japan charting the progress of The Great Village Campaign teams and challenging his listeners "to take another province for Christ." He was a strong believer in maps to help mission friends visualize the fields. In time, Cowman became known as "the man with the map."

Cowman's commitment to help direct the village campaign, while at the same time traveling abroad to fund the effort, soon translated into tremendous stress, a stress which eventually began to take a terrible toll. Early on, he experienced the first signs of heart trouble. Friends urged that they return home for a prolonged rest and recovery.

Cowman, while admitting his need for respite from the grueling pace, wrote to concerned friends, "I see no stopping place." Usually, after a brief recess, he would plunge back into the fray, "spending and being spent for Christ." For him, "let me burn out for thee, dear Lord," was more than a pious evangelical sentiment. It was a daily and inexorable reality. To fully understand the strategy and passion that drove these men to daily attempt the impossible dream (quixotic in the eyes of many missionary leaders), we must understand the very nature of this fledgling mission.

From the start, both Cowman and Kilbourne had a record of continual evangelization in the Chicago area and were motivated by this same urgent drive in Japan. "Evangelism" for them was far more than a spiritual word; it was the all-consuming blessed duty of continued work that exhibited itself in personal witness, daily distribution of literature, street meetings, and revival services. And, above all, it meant walking with the Gospel in hand to every town, every village, every soul.

Almost mind-boggling headlines appear in *The Missionary Standard* issue of 1914. Bold letters are emblazoned on the front page, "**3,000 CONTINUING NIGHTS!**" That was the length of time from the start of their work that evangelistic meetings had been held every evening in the Jimbo-Cho Gospel Hall. And as stated earlier, for the first 2,000 nights, they reported that there were seekers at the altar every evening but one. This incredible fact provides a window to the passion of men who undertook for Jesus efforts not only very nearly impossible but totally unreasonable in the eyes of others.

Chapter 6

YOUNG MEN OF THE CROSS

We have already spoken of the young volunteers, mostly with God's Bible School affiliation and from the Cincinnati area, who had come to Japan to assist the village campaigns. These intrepid young men were what we would call today short-term missionaries, although some eventually felt called to stay on for longer periods of time. Now in 1916, with the burden of completing the campaign strongly upon him, Cowman was inspired to challenge God's Bible School to recruit a team of their finest young men to help.

The target date for completion of the campaign had been set for the following year, December of 1917. As the date approached, however, it became obvious that in view of the limitations of both workers and funds, the 1917 date was unrealistic. As the men prayed, there came an inspiration. For years, during the Cowman's funding expeditions in the homeland, Charles and Lettie had made their headquarters either in Los Angeles or at God's Bible School in Cincinnati. The bulk of the OMS constituency and particularly friends, who had assisted the mission in its formative days, lived in the Chicago area or had ties with GBS in Cincinnati. Often during summer months, Charles and Lettie resided at the GBS campus and attended the school's famed camp meetings, probably the largest gathering of holiness adherents in the country. Popular speakers, such as Oswald Chambers, George D. Watson, Buddy Robinson, A.M. Hills, and Henry Morrison drew great crowds. On missionary day Charles and Lettie were often the featured speakers. Today it is frequently pointed out that the prominent GBS Administration Building still standing at the entry to the campus is where in 1900 Charles and Lettie had been called of God to Japan.

Very likely, during one of their brief furloughs at GBS, the Cowmans had been again impressed by the large number of young men full of enthusiasm and zeal to serve God. Many of them also demonstrated a great interest in missions. Why not, then, challenge a dozen or so of these young apostles to join OMS and Japanese evangelistic teams to complete the village campaigns. The plan was for them to spend a year with Japanese partners to walk the villages, mountains, fields and islands until the very last homes in Japan were reached. And what a difference this could make in the lives of every one of these noble men. The idea caught fire. Once Cowman had presented his vision and obtained the approval of GBS President Dr. Meredith D. Standley, they were free to proceed.

Almost as soon as the word was out, applications began to come from student volunteers. It was decided that candidates must be mature, experienced in Christian service, and preferably upper classmen. Faculty members and Sister Knapp, widow of GBS founder Martin Wells Knapp, helped with recruitment, approaching students that they considered zealous and well suited to the demands and rigors of the task. Upon completion of the year in Japan, the young men if not already graduates would be expected to return to GBS to complete their schooling. It was also agreed that the optimum number for the GBS team would be ten.

As recruitment proceeded, the prospect of GBS' young evangelists joining the historic crusade generated great interest. The school began by referring to the volunteers as the school's "splendid young men." OMS magazine articles dubbed them, "wonderful young boys." Blackstone, a long-time friend of OMS and supporter of the campaign, upon learning of the final thrust, offered to pay all of the GBS boys' expenses for the entire year, including travel.

During the final months of 1916 leading up to the young men's departure for Japan, testimonies and biographical material began to appear in the pages of the GBS magazine, *God's Revivalist*. In one issue was a handsome double-spread studio portrait of the team, the boys smartly standing shoulder to shoulder—all except Harry Woods who was already in the pastorate. The boys' names and a brief bio appear in the school's 2001 centennial publication, "God's Clock Keeps Perfect Time."

Lewis Kyles, 30 years of age, was from Glassboro, New Jersey. He had attended a Bible school in North Carolina for two years before going to GBS. He graduated in 1916, started to preach but said he felt impressed to return to GBS for further study. "I actually returned without notifying the trustees that I was coming," he said. "But they kindly allowed me to enroll." When the call came for workers in Japan, "I jumped at the chance."

John Orkney from Ramon, Washington, had heard both Cowman and Kilbourne speak of their missionary work. He was a student at GBS in 1916 when Edward Oney returned to the campus to help recruit others for The Great Village Campaign. John was 24 and he later married Anna May Neff, sister to Paul Haines's wife, Myrtle.

Rollie Poe from Lexington, Kentucky, was 24 in 1916 and, though from a Christian home, he had rebelled against his godly upbringing. At his mother's death bed, he had promised that he would meet her in heaven, a promise he promptly forgot. Later, a friend invited him to the Wilmore, Kentucky, Camp Meeting. "After a tremendous battle," he recalled, "I finally surrendered to God. He took me, a boy who had been a rebel, and made me an heir of God and a joint-heir with Jesus Christ." Shortly thereafter, he was sanctified and enrolled in GBS where he worked in the Revivalist Press. When the call came for evangelists in Japan, he was not slow to respond.

William Miller, destined to become a well-known Nazarene evangelist, was born in Oklahoma in what he described as Indian territory. "I had ungodly parents," he said. "I don't remember either one of them praying, not once." His mother died when he was 11 but received Christ on her death bed. "Life was dark for me," he said. "My associates were wicked men, cowboys, Indians and bootleggers. I learned from them and served the devil." In 1912, William went to Alaska. En route home he visited an uncle in Spokane, Washington. "I had never been in a home like that," he said. "There were Bible mottos on the walls in every room. Evenings, they had family devotions. About that time a revival was scheduled in my uncle's church. I went to the altar. A week later behind the old school house, I told Jesus three times that I loved Him. A landslide of glory struck my soul and a huge burden of sin rolled away. That was November 20, 1912. Later while working in a lumber camp, the Lord called me to preach."

Miller had very little schooling. Nevertheless, he applied to God's Bible School. They permitted him to help in the Revival Press part time while taking classes. Thus he worked his way through school. When the call came for volunteers to Japan, William, the bold, rough-hewn zealot and a natural leader, determined to join and help finish the village campaign.

Vernie Stanley was from High Point, North Carolina, and at 22 the youngest member of the team. Vern grew up in a Christian home but at 14 ran away and began drinking. He fell ill, repented, and promised God that he would serve him. But it was a promise he did not keep. In August 1914, he again ran away from home, lied about his age and enlisted in the army. After spending some time in the Philippines, he was shipped to China. "There," he says, "God caught up with me; conviction seized me. I could not eat or sleep. Where will I spend eternity? was the question that tormented me day and night. My parents sent a request to GBS to pray for me. I finally was saved in the home of a missionary in China. But then I again fell into sin. When I was discharged, I went home and was reclaimed. I enrolled in GBS where Brother Oney urged me to join the other young men going to Japan. I volunteered and was accepted."

Everett Williamson was from Amanda, Ohio, and age 29 in 1917. He grew up in an old-fashioned Methodist home but wandered away from the Lord. He began to pray and seek God in 1910. After contracting typhoid fever, he repented and was called to preach in 1913 after visiting a camp meeting with his pastor. He enrolled in GBS as a "work student." After sanctification, there came a powerful impulse to serve God as a missionary.

Paul Haines came from a godly home in nearby Dayton, Ohio. He enrolled in GBS, graduated in 1916, and accepted a pastorate. Sister Knapp contacted him and urged him to join the other GBS students bound for Japan. He later married Myrtle Neff and together they spent most of their lives with OMS in Korea and then at mission headquarters in Los Angeles where Paul served as treasurer.

Edward Oney was the first of the GBS students to enlist. He had earlier, in 1914, left GBS to join the Cowmans in Japan. In 1916 the Cowmans sent him back to Cincinnati to recruit other students for The Great Village Campaign.

William Thiele was from Idaho and raised in a devout Methodist home. "My parents frequently entertained clergymen," he remembers. "At first I liked preachers but later on grew uncomfortable in their presence and tried to avoid them. I fought conviction for years. A voice seemed to say 'If you go to the altar you will have to be a preacher'." He finally yielded and was saved in 1912, after which he enrolled in God's Bible School for three years before joining the village campaign.

Harry Woods came from a family of 14 and was the son of a well-known preacher and evangelist, John Woods, from West Virginia. Harry from early childhood was very devout and was sometimes teased by his family and friends who dubbed him the "Little Deacon." He enrolled in God's Bible School in 1912 and left in 1914 to take a pastorate. In 1916 he received a letter from Sister Knapp urging him to join the team of ten young men going to Japan. "After praying over it," he said, "I consented to go." He and Paul Haines were destined to join OMS and spend many years in the Orient.

Chapter 7

FINAL PREPARATIONS

Once the ten young evangelists had been recruited, they made preparations to leave for Japan in January, 1917. From the pages of *God's Revivalist* as well as a GBS centennial article by Larry Smith, we find the following record of the boys during their final days prior to sailing for Japan:

> As the boys packed their luggage, solemnity seemed to hover over the campus family which felt keenly God moving in their midst. In the old wooden tabernacle, a thrilling farewell service was conducted on Sunday, December 24. Missionary hymns were sung. Each of the boys gave his testimony. Then Brother Schell, on behalf of the college, bade them an eloquent and sincere "Farewell." The boys waved from the platform and the audience responded with waving hands and handkerchiefs.

Although Dr. Blackstone in California covered the entire expense of this band of sanctified and consecrated young men, *God's Revivalist* noted that funds were still needed for such expenses as 552,500 Gospels and tracts that would be distributed.

All were well in body and soul when they arrived in Los Angeles by train in early January. The amazed conductor reported that he "had never carried such a crowd before as they sang hymns most of the way."

The boys reported that in Los Angeles on Saturday they had the privilege of visiting Charles Cowman's father, "very frail and ready at any moment to enter through the gates of pearl." He had been eagerly looking forward to living to greet them, and God gave him his heart's desire so that he was able to sit up and shake hands with each one.

Praise God. On Sabbath they began services in Trinity Missionary Church, the only Apostolic Holiness Church (later renamed The Pilgrim Holiness Church) on the coast. Then the fire began to fall when the missionary band sang "Here am I, Lord, send me." And how the Lord did bless the young men as they gave their testimonies. There was scarcely a dry eye in the room.

The afternoon services were held at Dr. Watson's church, and it reminded one of an old-fashioned camp meeting. The fire fell again and there was a shout in the camp; the missionary fire had a tremendous kindling. The evening service was held again in the Trinity Church, and God made it the crowning meeting of the day. The Holy Spirit moved mightily and seven young men and women were at the altar. The meeting closed at 11 p.m. None can ever forget that blessed Sabbath day—oh, it was wonderful! God was in our midst, in such mighty power. It was unmistakably a divine seal on their going.

Another farewell service for the young men was held in Oakland on Tuesday night, and Wednesday afternoon the steamer "Korea" sailed away with the precious band on board. Seventeen days later they marched down the gangplank in Yokohama. The devil and his angels are waiting for a hand-to-hand contest against Christ and His soldiers, but our captain Jesus is leading His own hosts and He will speedily conquer. The villages that have waited hundreds of years shall hear the joyful tidings, "Salvation full and free." Glory to God!

We mean to press right into every dark village and into every heathen home till the whole of Japan has been covered with the knowledge of Jesus. Until then, we dare not rest. God's call to our hearts is onward, onward, and with His help we are obeying. Someday we shall hear the summons onward and the gates of heaven will open and we shall enter here. But until then, the call is to the work, to the

> work. We are servants of God. Let us follow the path that our Master hath trod.

When the boys arrived in Japan, they were temporarily housed in the homes of missionaries on the campus of the Bible school. Here they, no doubt, saw copies of the final 1916 issue of *The Missionary Standard*. As though to celebrate their arrival of the GBS Ten and the launching of their heroic endeavor, the magazine reiterated the goal of the coming year. In bold letters at the top of the page was "VISITING EVERY HOME IN JAPAN" and then Kilbourne's words:

> A STRIKING CAMPAIGN NOW IN PROGRESS
>
> You may ask, "Tell me about this village campaign in which OMS is now engaged. What is the object and plan? What do you propose doing and what will likely be the results?" These are questions arising in the minds of many of the homeland saints because they have seen that it is something of a departure from the regular lines of missionary work and a new venture, so to speak, in modern missions.
>
> In replying to these questions, we wish first of all to speak of the inspiring element that caused us to begin this ministry. It was, in brief, a strong desire that laid hold upon us to literally fulfill the great commission, to go to every creature. We were brought face to face with the fact that after 50 years of missionary effort in Japan the great masses of the population living in the rural districts are utterly untouched by the Gospel. Nearly four-fifths of the empire unevangelized will never be reached unless someone goes to them. These things came home to our hearts and minds with such force that we were humiliated before God and led to cry to Him for an explanation and a remedy.
>
> It seems to us that He gave us the plans as we again reconsidered the commission: "Go ye into all the world and preach the Gospel to every creature." These words lit up

with new meaning and with that came a new responsibility. When we considered the word “go,” we began to realize that it meant more than we had ever thought. There is no promise in the Word that would lead us to believe the lost will come to us for the Gospel in this dispensation. So we began slowly to realize what in our going to “every creature” was involved, and it would mean going in the very literal sense. If the atonement covers every creature, as we all believe, then we owe it to every individual to bring the good tidings to them. We certainly believe that Jesus meant this when giving the commission so what right have we to disregard it in its expressed literal meaning? Hence, “going” began to mean much more to us and a systematic house-to-house campaign was begun from our Jerusalem (Tokyo) outward. We have now covered more than half of Japan and over 5,000,000 homes have been visited.

And now as to the object, you have already surmised from the foregoing that it is to actually visit every home in Japan and bring to them some knowledge of salvation, to place within their reach something that will, if they desire to know, enlighten them concerning God, sin, Jesus, salvation, and the other fundamentals of Christianity. The printed matter used is some part of the Scriptures, either a Gospel or a portion of selected Scripture, together with a simple Gospel tract. These two bound together are handed in at each door by our colporteurs.

But this is only a part of the object for we fully realize that the distribution of salvation literature alone is not enough. We want men and women to repent and believe and get really converted so this requires a more definite and determined ministry. This is made possible by having as colporteurs men who know how to lead souls to Christ. We have only one object in view and that is to get people saved. Our evangelists know how to tactfully make use of their opportunities to testify; they are men who can pray through every difficulty; who know how to conduct a street march and preach either in the street or hall; who know how to meet the civil authorities and put every agency to work to help the campaign. God is giving us this class of men. We have printed hundreds of incidents to show that results do follow, and you may read others in this issue.

As to the plan, it involves sending out bands of Japanese workers under the leadership of a missionary or experienced native leader to work two-by-two from a common center. Systematically, township by township, county by county, province by province, the evangelists proceed until the whole land has been filled with the Gospel. Names and addresses of all converts and seekers are taken and sent in to headquarters to be recorded and cared for by correspondence or by sending other Christian literature. Hungry hearts are all about us in this ripe land, and there are many ways in which we may do them good if we are alive and awake. Wherever there is found an evangelical church, cooperation is sought, and the names of converts from that district are given to the pastor.

Beloved, Japan needs your help, first by your prayers. Pray that the printed page may be lit up by the Holy Ghost; the right kind of men be raised up to help the seekers; that they become truly converted and follow the Lord; that the homeland saints from north, south, east, and west may be stirred up to pray and give; that God will prosper every effort and make the Word living and active; that we may be enabled to see quickly the accomplishments of this work in Japan in order that we may proceed to other fields. We are certain that the Lord of the harvest desires this kind of work done throughout the Orient.

Then, Japan needs your help in offerings. No matter how poor we may be God will not deny us the blessed privilege of giving something, even out of our poverty. It is the pennies that make up the dollars—every one counts. Some have given sufficient for a whole province and others who are able have given large amounts, but we are satisfied that God is going to let His little ones who are poor as regards to earthly possessions have the privilege of doing the major part of the work. Then again you can help by stirring others to give by handing out literature, passing on the paper, and praying conviction on indifferent ones. God needs the whole army of saints to go up against this Jericho, and every reader should stand in His place and help push the message of the glorious Gospel into the remotest corners of dark, yet ripe, Japan.

Kneel right down, beloved, as the Lord is speaking to you and, before the holy impression dies away, ask Him what He would have you do and send your offerings to the address found on page six.

(In a box adjacent to this article and in bold print is the following:)

Are you too poor to give? Then, pray. Have you but a little to give? Withhold it not. Have you much to give? You cannot find a better investment. Remember that it is the $1, the $5, the $10 and the $100 that have made it possible to do the village campaign work. God wants all of you to have a share in it.

Charles Cowman with his parents and sister – 1901

Charles Cowman at age 5

Charles' mother at age 78

Charles and Lettie newlyweds
June 8, 1889

Charles about the time of his call

Juji Nakada with family.
His mother was one of Japan's earliest Christians.

Charles and Lettie in Japan
1911

Cowmans and Kilbournes with workers in front of the mission hall in Tokyo.

Sandal shop, Tokyo

Vegetable market, Tokyo

Typical Japanese village – circa 1920

Japanese hand tram

Jin-rickshaws, primary mode of transportation - Japan 1903

Women's meeting, Tokyo, top far R: Julia Kilbourne – circa 1912

Cowman at his desk, Tokyo

Juji Nakada, front row center, with Bible school students – circa 1910

1913 Japan Holiness Church convention; 2nd row (L-5 to R), Juji Nakada, Verna Herlzler, Julia and E.A. Kilbourne, Mr. and Mrs. John Thomas, Tetsusaburo Sasao, Bud Kilbourne, Lizzie Pearce, Minnie Upperman

God's Bible School camp meeting – circa 1916
Charles and Lettie Cowman, third row

Chapter 8

HOW SHALL THEY HEAR?

In the same issue of the magazine, Ernest Kilbourne in his editorial, and characteristically eloquent fashion, addresses a question that has troubled many. He writes:

> A young Japanese man when spoken to about his soul's salvation said, "You must not blame me. I do not know any better. I've never heard before. No one has preached me a missionary sermon that has gone right home to my heart and stirred up all the memories of past failures and impressed me to obey the great commission and give His Gospel to every creature."
>
> Now this is not a new message but coming to us from the inspired Word of God with a fresh sword thrust. It is a hard blow; it cuts deep; it brings blood but it should cause the true soldier of the cross to take a firmer grip on the sword of the Spirit and go into the fray seeking the deliverance of precious souls.
>
> Consider the young man's words: "You must not blame me." His point is well taken for first of all the heathen has a right to place the blame for his ignorance of the Gospel somewhere else than himself. He is not to blame. That is a fact and we can't deny it. The very fact that we are commissioned to go into all the world and preach the Gospel to every creature carries with it the acknowledgment that the whole world is in ignorance of these glad tidings, and we are the ones to be blamed if the great commission is unfulfilled.
>
> One may argue, if they please, that the salvation or damnation of the heathen hangs upon a very slender thread if it is dependent upon the Christian witnessing to every

creature in the world. But our argument falls to the ground when faced with the oft-repeated words of Jesus commissioning His disciples and equipping them for this very task: "Ye shall be my witnesses unto the uttermost part of the earth." They and the early church went everywhere and preached the Gospel, and these glad tidings became known to their world. Now it is incumbent on us to do the same.

His second argument is "No one has preached me a message that has stirred my heart." Perhaps the young man is a worshipper of evil spirits. When he hears of the Almighty who is stronger than the devil and who came to destroy his works, he takes refuge behind his ignorance. "I do not know any better." Oh, the pathos of those words. You may argue that he ought to have seen God in creation and the beauties of nature. But let me tell you, beloved, that for the most part the things the heathen sees in nature are not its beauty but the deviltries of the carnal nature. They are constantly in contact with the lowest forms of bestiality or the needs for constant struggle for daily bread. These harsh realities shut out all the beauties of nature, even if such might reveal God. But in the event that they rise above their depressing surroundings and see the hand of an Almighty Creator, who is going to tell them of the mediator Jesus Christ, the only name, the only Savior, they still say, "I do not know any better."

St. Paul asks the question: "How shall he ever hear without a preacher?" The winds and the waves testify but heathen usually see only demon power. There is only one voice which can enlighten the heathen soul, and that is the voice of the Holy Ghost from the Spirit-filled Gospel messenger who has gone into all the world and preached the Gospel to every creature in obedience to the Great Commission of our Lord. God Almighty have mercy upon us if we hide behind some man-made excuse for not going to the lost with the message of the “Lamb of God which takes away the sin of the world.”

Beloved, there are almost a thousand million souls who can stand up as this young man did and point their fingers at us and say, “You must not blame me. I do not know any better. I have never heard.” Do you not see those fingers pointing right at you just now? Well, thank God some of us may truly answer “I have done what I could.” But, oh, how many there are who must shrink back before that searching finger that accuses “Thou art the man.” You who know Christ have done little or nothing to give them the Gospel. You must bear the blame and that makes us guilty of their blood. Let us resolve that by the grace of God we will give ourselves for the salvation of all souls until Jesus comes. Amen.

Chapter 9

EARLY DAYS

On the completion of their orientation, the ten young men from God's Bible School were all assigned to the various Gospel teams. Each of these teams had five national workers, all OMS Bible school graduates who had proven effective in evangelism and soul-winning. Some of these had a smattering of English and were, to some degree, able to translate for the young Americans. For the most part, however, the preaching was done entirely in Japanese by men who spoke it as their mother tongue.

Although in later years the Gospel teams were housed in tents, at this time they were lodged either in inns or in rooms adjacent to the Gospel halls. As for beds, the Japanese have always preferred to sleep on the floor on a grass mat called a tatami. In cool weather they cover themselves with quilts which they call futons. For Americans accustomed to spring mattresses or feather beds, these "innovations" took some getting used to.

Upon arrival in a village or town, the first order of the day was a march and an invitation to the evening service. At the same time, members of the team moved among the gathering crowd to pass out handbills, announcing the location and time of the meetings. In the July *God's Revivalist,* William Miller has a lively account of his first days in Japanese villages. Under the heading of "From One of the Ten," he writes:

> I shall never forget the time when we boys stepped aboard the steamship in San Francisco. As the old ship began to move from the dear land we love so much and as many people were crowded about the shore bidding friends and loved ones goodbye, we boys stood on the upper deck along the railing watching the new scenes. Oh, how the mighty omnipotent presence of God illuminated our hearts. Truly, God was with us and He made it easy. We long to go

> where we know we are in His sweet will, representing the One who has commissioned us to go and tell the good tidings to others.
>
> God gave us excellent weather and we landed safe in the sunrise kingdom January 20. We were 17 days on the sea but each day was a day of victory. We landed with a zeal and determination to spread the Gospel like Samson's foxes spread the fire.

Then describing the beginning of The Great Village Campaign, Miller writes:

> When we reached the village, we held a street meeting. I preached on the true remedy for sin and how we might obtain joy and peace. After the meeting, we told all that wished to obtain this experience to come to our hotel which was about two blocks away. Scores followed us.
>
> We crowded 31 into our rooms. The hallways were also filled and there was a crowd on the outside. Oh, how the Shekinah glory did fill the old heathen hotel and how Jesus melted hard hearts. As our Japanese team members talked to them, big tears rolled down their cheeks, and many left with Jesus crowned king of kings in their hearts. To God be all the glory. Sadly, we had to go on and leave the little crowd there without anyone to look after them because we did not have enough workers.

The daily routine, of course, consisted for the most part of what the Japanese call "haifu," distribution of the plan of salvation in Gospel literature to every home in the area. Miller writes of one of his haifu treks:

> That day I was working in the mountains and came to a large village of about 500 houses. As I passed a school, I gave the principal a Gospel portion and told him it was the book of the living and true God. I went on down the street

giving out my tracts when I heard someone calling. I looked around and here came the principal. He could speak a little English. He asked me if I was a Christian and I told him that I was. He said, "I want you to come into the school and teach Christianity. We are so hungry to hear more about it." But, as I could not speak the Japanese language and he could not speak enough English to interpret for me, I had to go on.

Later I met an old lady as she was coming from the mountains. I had passed her home and given her a Gospel portion telling of the way of life. She then followed me three miles desiring to know more. Oh, how she did talk in her language which I did not understand. Even so it was clear that she was hungry for God. When I met one of my Japanese helpers, I told him to testify to the woman. She stood with her heart opened, receiving every word he said. As we left she stated that she would seek the true God until she found Him.

In the same issue of *God's Revivalist* is a letter from Brother Orkney:

My initial work in the villages of Japan was on February 1, 1917. The first few days were times of great joy to my soul as I gave out Gospel portions in Hyogo Province. There was a great festival of some kind going on in that place when we arrived, the streets so crowded with people making it almost impossible for us to get through. I saw many things which caused me to rejoice in my mission and feel that I had a great privilege granted to me of God to help such benighted people to see the light of the Gospel of Christ. Oh, how my heart has gone out to God since I have seen the needs of these people.

In places as I gave out the Gospel portions, the faces of the people would light up and they would thank me heartily. Now we are on the island of Kyushu. We had a most precious time here yesterday. God's presence was felt in the prayer meeting, both morning and evening, and He was also present as I talked to Him in the afternoon.

While we were in prayer in the native inn, the keeper came up and listened to us pray and worship God. He stayed out in the adjoining room for a while, kneeling and listening to us pray. We invited him in and my boys read, expounded the scriptures, and prayed with him. By the expression on his face, it was clear that God was talking to him. In the evening while we were praying before starting for the street meeting, I saw another man with the innkeeper standing at the top of the stairs. They were listening intently. Praise God, there is a divine work going on in this place.

Our open-air meeting was splendid. Several times during the day I asked the Lord to give us something special to encourage our hearts and to help some precious soul. Glory to our Christ, He answered prayer.

The boys sang and two of them preached. Then I sang "The Old Rugged Cross" in English. How it blessed my soul. After singing, I began to testify and the Lord wonderfully helped me. I had neither interpreter nor interrupter. As I talked away, God's spirit was upon me, and, although nobody understood English, the crowd began to gather. The only words I could say in Japanese were "hontono kamisana," which means "true God." And He wonderfully undertook.

We walked up and down the streets for a while and then approached the railroad station. One of the boys who works there heard us. His father is a Christian. After supper, the boy telephoned us that he wanted to talk with us concerning salvation. After about two hours' time with him, my men say that he has been blessedly saved. Hallelujah! Praise the Lord! He may now join our bands to help distribute the Gospel. He is a fine-looking and robust young man.

Orkney concludes his letter with:

> I am thinking today that if God continues to bless me in spirit, soul and body as He has this past month the hardest thing of all will be for me to leave and go back to the States again after this village work is completed.

For the recent arrivals from the United States, the early days of distribution in the villages were a challenge to say the least. Harry Woods reports:

> Everywhere we went into every village, no matter how small, we found heathenism, either in the form of a temple or a shrine. As we heard the tolling of the temple bells and observed the superstition and idolatry of this poor benighted people, our souls cried out to God. How we pray that as the printed portions of the Gospel are read by the people the Holy Ghost will use them to enlighten their souls and bring them to the knowledge of salvation. Oh, that the church will awaken to the great responsibility of the commission given by our Savior.
>
> This work has not been the easiest to accomplish. It has cost some life blood of those engaged in it. Many times after treading over mountains all day have we come in with tired, aching bodies and blistered feet; at other times we are very wet, having worked in the rain all day.
>
> On one occasion our strength was utterly exhausted. That day we had to cross several very large mountains, one especially high, to visit five villages. It was almost five o'clock in the evening when the last point was reached. Then we had to again traverse these same mountains, a distance of about 11 miles, to get back to the inn where we were staying. We had safely crossed all the mountains, except the last and highest one, when our strength gave out completely. We tried to go farther but try as hard as we

> could we could not. By this time it was dark with no one around to help us. Exhausted we lay down beside the mountain trail and immediately fell asleep. We slept for about 30 minutes when suddenly we awoke and found ourselves crying unto the Lord for strength. This was graciously given to us, and we were able to reach the top of the mountain and safely descend to the other side, reaching the native inn at 9:10 p.m.
>
> In all my experiences, I have found His grace to be sufficient and count it a great privilege to labor for Him in this ripe and needy field. Indeed, after we have done all, as Jesus said, confess that we are unprofitable servants in that our very best efforts fail to repay the Father for all He has done for us. Pray for me that I may be a faithful soldier of the cross.

It did not take long for the boys to realize the epochal difficulties of the task they had undertaken. Paul Haines in his autobiography gives us a lively description of all that was involved in seeking to literally place God's Word in every home in Japan. He starts with a narrative of their farewell in Los Angeles:

> In Los Angeles, we were invited to an upscale restaurant for the farewell dinner. Upon introducing us to the proprietor, Mr. Cowman told him that these boys were destined to travel through Japan to place the Gospel in every home of the Japanese empire and that they would be living native style all the way: eating native food, sleeping on the floor, bathing in Japanese fashion. The restaurant owner exclaimed: "Oh, that would be wonderful. I'd pay $500 for an experience like that." Later this man's words frequently came to mind, especially when I was struggling to eat a breakfast of fish and rice that involved picking morsels of meat from the fish's gills while seeing the fish's bright eyeballs looking up at me. That same day for lunch I was served bitter Japanese tea without cream or sugar, along with gritty food at an open roadside stand. Back at

> the inn that night, we had a bowl of soup containing the same fish head that I had countenanced that morning. The eyes, I learned, had been consumed by my fellow evangelists. The thought came to me during that dismal meal, I wonder if our restaurant friend in Los Angeles would be willing to pay $500 for an experience like this!
>
> And then there was the ecstasy of sleeping under a dark and heavy mosquito net on a hot summer night, hummed to sleep by an orchestra of the little creatures swarming around us in droves and seeking entrance through the holes in the net of which there were quite a few. Added to this was the pleasure of the company of armies of fleas which left me well tattooed. In the morning, I looked like I had a severe case of measles all the way from my neck to my ankles. Again the thought, I wonder if for this delightful experience our restaurant friend would have been willing to fork out $500. And then, of course, was the daily pleasure of hiking. Vehicles were seldom available to us and our mode of travel for those 300 days a year was on shanks mares. We averaged between 15 and 25 miles a day. During these long, tedious days of continual tramp, tramp, tramp, plodding through mud, up mountains, small trails and village paths, as I thought of our restaurant friend, I mused that perhaps he would be willing to give much more than $500 just to escape the delights of our mission.

Some, upon learning of the GBS boys' goal of reaching literally every home, had questions as to the possibility of actually accomplishing this. Haines writes that, of course, it is meant that a sincere effort was made to as far as humanly possible reach every home. In these early days of the formation of the Japanese military, maps could be obtained by anyone upon request. Thus there was available the layout of whole counties, towns, villages and streets. As for rural areas, usually even the most distant and isolated homes could be located and approximate mileage given. It should be admitted, however, that in some areas accurate maps were not available, and one had to inquire of local citizens as to how to find remote dwellings. At times the team members themselves saw barely-visible thatched roofs on distant mountain slopes. Despite all the interminable walking, the weariness, and the utter fatigue, the richest prize of the day's long hours was leading precious souls to the fountain of life.

To those who charged that the mere distribution of tracts to the homes of Japan was at best a superficial work hardly worth the effort, Paul Haines explains:

> Our men upon returning to the inn in the evening or afternoon would hold open-air services on street corners where hundreds heard the Gospel proclaimed and seekers were dealt with by our national evangelists. If there were any churches in the area, all names and addresses of inquirers were turned over to local pastors and then copies of the same were sent to mission headquarters in Tokyo. Additional literature, Bibles, Testaments, and other booklets and tracts were made available upon request. For some years after the campaign was completed, a veritable mail-order business was carried on to provide inquirers with literature they requested. To this, I should add that frequently our band members found opportunity to do "special evangelism," bringing seekers to the inn for counsel after meetings. Where the result was a group of believers, a small church was formed and pastored by a recent graduate of our Tokyo seminary. No small volume would be required to present all the wonderful experiences in soul winning by both missionary and national workers.

Chapter 10

THE AINU

One province assigned to the GBS boys was the great northern island of Hokkaido with a population at that time of over 2,000,000. The weather is extremely cold in winter and snow very deep so that only during the summer months could work be done there. "This island," one of the evangelists writes, "is home to the Ainu, the early inhabitants of Japan. Their history presents a most fascinating study, and there seems little doubt that they come from the same stock as North American Indians. It is also a little known fact that prior to the arrival of the Ainus, Japan was inhabited by a race of dwarfs whom the Ainus supplanted. These small creatures lived in caves and pits and were called 'earth spiders.' They were ousted from the mainland but in the Kurile Islands, just across a small stretch of sea, are remnants of this race. The Ainu, however, have survived and can be seen today in their still primitive state in the interior of Hokkaido."

In their determination to reach every soul with the Gospel, the boys hiked to a remote interior area where several families of Ainu remained. This was more than 32 miles from the nearest railway, and the first 15 miles were covered by riding a primitive horse-drawn carriage after which they walked the desolate moor to a tiny fishing village. From there, they traveled by horseback for 17 more miles through forests of oak, lime, chestnut and birch. The village street, at first glance, did not look unlike any ordinary Japanese village, but it was noticed that the distant roofs were thatched with rushes and the walls were also woven of rushes. There were no chimneys in these houses, but a small hole in the west angle of the roof allowed smoke to escape. It was not considered polite to look into a hut through the south window and positively an insult to look in the east window thought to be peculiarly sacred. The people were very superstitious in this regard and often worshipped facing the sunrise through the east window, taking care not to desecrate it in any way. Haines explained:

These people, primitive as they are, do not take kindly to crimes of theft or burglary. The punishment for the first offense is a sound beating. For the second, sometimes the nose is cut off, sometimes the ears, and sometimes both! Persons who commit such crimes twice are driven out of the village to which they belonged.

The Ainu live primarily by hunting. Their weapons are bow and arrow, spear, and a short sword. For bear and deer hunting, they use poisoned arrows which in a short time paralyze their prey, rendering them easy to dispatch. Bear and deer are now so nearly exterminated that the people have to depend on other animals for food. Intermarriage is another cause for the diminishing of the Ainus. Cold and exposure take a regular toll and murderous night raids have often wiped out whole villages. And, finally, the intense longing for intoxicating drink is eating out the life of the people. Their religious rites involve orgies of drunkenness. No ceremony is complete without intoxicants, and festivals only reach their climax when men fall in a stupor.

The Ainu people are not handsome and the average height of a man is about five feet four inches. Yet there is something impressive in their strength and dignity. Their most striking feature is their fine hair and thick beard. Ainu women are, in their way, as picturesque as the men. Their curious feature is a tattoo a little below the lower lip. This is not done all at once. The first touch is applied when still a youth. Then year by year it is extended until in late life reaches almost from ear to ear. We read in Revelation 7:9 of a great multitude of all nations and kindreds and people and tongues that will stand before the throne with white robes. Certainly there will be Ainu among them.

The Cincinnati God's Bible School community had been kept well informed as to the progress of the village campaign, and many had pledged to pray for the men daily. Readers of *God's Revivalist* were also intently following the progress of the boys in Japan and bearing them daily before the throne of grace. One such reader was Lucy Crippen. She wrote to Lettie Cowman:

> My precious Sister in Jesus, My soul is thrilled with the joy over what our wonderful band has accomplished, moving through Japan with a portion of God's word in every home. Jesus wakes me early in the morning to focus on the boys and pray. I have been asking Him to fill the place left by my precious only son. He leaped to his death from a fourth-story hotel window in Lancaster. When his father reached the pavement, our dear son had gotten up and was leaning over a box groaning. His father put his arm around him and walked him back to the room. He lived five hours. When Jesus revealed to me that now I have ten precious "sons" who went from the "mount of blessings," I leaped from my bed filled with heavenly dynamite. Hallelujah! I believe this is just the way it will be when Jesus comes for His bride. When I read the boys' reports, it makes me think that they are like my precious boy. Will there not be a time in heaven when these boys meet my Charlie and tell him what they have done? I will be there to rejoice with them. Glory to God . . . I am sending you a $10 money order to help finish the work. Will it not be grand when a nation is born in a day and Satan chained and locked up a thousand years? I am so happy that I can hardly stay in this world. Your sister in Jesus, Lucy Crippen.

Chapter 11

TRANSFORMED LIVES

The readers of *God's Revivalist*, as well as *The Missionary Standard* were kept advised of the boys' progress by way of maps. In the September 1917 issue of *The Standard*, on the front page, is the map of Japan showing seven yet unreached areas. Cowman writes:

> This map will show our readers the progress of The Great Village Campaign since its last appearance in these pages. There remain seven provinces including the Looju Islands (Okinawa) yet to be visited. With our present forces, they can be finished in a few months, and every home will have a portion of the Word of God and a Gospel tract—a ray of light, a chance for salvation, a message from Jesus to every creature in this ripe harvest field. Let us continue to water this precious seed of the heavenly kingdom with our tears and prayers, and it shall continue to yield its harvest.

The target date for the completion of The Great Village Campaign was first the end of 1917 and then moved to January 1918. The tens of thousands of homes still waiting to be visited before the boys returned to God's Bible School did not allow for the leisure of staying in any one area very long, either to make friends or evangelize. Of course, language limitations made it difficult for them to be involved in a great deal of personal work. Nevertheless, quite amazing, the record of the young evangelists in *The Missionary Standard* and *God's Revivalist* tells repeatedly of the instances when limited contacts along with the distribution of Gospel literature led to wonderful and almost instant response. Everett Williamson reports:

> Yesterday I was too sick to work or read or get hold of God in prayer, and this morning did not feel much better in

body. In fact, I thought I was worse, but the Lord was working. Brother Niura, my leading worker, was up early and I heard him out on the porch praying. I got up and prayed, too, and felt that the Lord wanted me to go to work so I told the boys I was going to work in the town. After a breakfast of hot milk and toast and a good prayer meeting, we started out. As the day wore on, my strength increased.

We arrived in this town at a special time. On this day they were holding a heathen festival. People were here from far and near. It is similar to our county fair at home. I call it "the devil's camp meeting," because of the fakirs and like who are trying to get money off the people. They have a race course also. While the devil is trying to give the people his wares, we slip the Word of God in everywhere.

Just before dinner, I got around to the temple and gave a Gospel portion to the priest's son. As I left he came running after me and invited me back. I returned and I talked with him. I told him that God had forgiven my sins and given me such joy that I had come from America to Japan to tell the Japanese about Jesus. With his limited English he said that although his father was a Buddhist he was turning to Christianity. He then went with me and told the people about the book which I was giving them and urged them to read it. The people seemed to wonder why he was giving out a Christian book rather than Buddhist literature. But he assured them it was good and true and told them to read it.

In Cowman and Kilbourne's report on The Great Village Campaign, they write:

After campaign workers placed the Gospel in homes of the people in Yamanashi, they came to a small town on the slope of Mt. Fuji. Here, too, they prayerfully placed Gospel portions in each house. They met a man who was a slave to drink and sin and was said to be "the worst character in town," and the cause of much trouble. However, the Lord was mindful of him. A Gospel portion fell into his hand, showing him his sinful condition and convicting him so deeply that he could not rest. He came to our workers and they taught him more about the plan of salvation. But he was not satisfied and could not pray through. Yet, God continued to work in his heart. He finally came to Tokyo to inquire again as to how he might be saved. Juji Nakada prayed with him and led him to Christ. What a wonderful change came into that life. He turned away from his sins and his old companions and started out with a fixed determination to serve God and witness to His saving power.

The wife of this brother was so impressed with the change in his life that she, too, decided to seek the Lord. After that, the mother who had long been a strict Buddhist also turned to the Lord followed by her two daughters. Others also began to notice the change in this family and inquired as to the cause. The brother wrote to our office in Tokyo earnestly requesting that we send a preacher of the Gospel to his town, promising to pay the rent for the mission and contribute to the preacher's allowance.

God was working, too, and made it possible for us to send a worker right away. During the past few months he has had the joy of seeing a group of about 50 or 60 men and women turn from darkness to light. He is continually testifying about what God has done for him.

Oh, brother and sister, Edwin (Bud) Kilbourne recently visited this mission and spent a weekend there. He was greatly encouraged to see the manifestation of God's work. One of two daughters feels called to become a Bible woman and hopes to enter the Bible training institute before long. Who can tell what will be the end result of one Gospel portion? According to God's promise, "His word shall not return unto Him void."

In the October issue of *God's Revivalist*, Cowman gives another heartening account:

> In Brother Thiele's band is a native worker named Brother Arkai, a precious man with a great burden for lost souls. Recently, instead of coming back from Gospel distribution at six in the evening, he would lose track of time. Often he would return at eight and nine and sometimes later. The only explanation he gave to the team leader, Brother Thiele, was a report of all God was doing. Then he would tumble in to his bed on the floor for a few hours before rising early and starting off for another day. Recently, at one home he visited, the owner was standing in his garden and called to him. "Come in," he said. "We wish to hear this teaching." The brother happily complied and the whole family was summoned to listen. Then the man said, "When I was a mere lad, I heard this story just once and I have often wished to hear it again but no one has ever come our way."
>
> Brother Arkai spent several hours in the home, patiently telling them the story of redeeming love. The master broke down in tears and prayed, "Oh, God, for years I've longed to know you. Please, save me." Others in the family were also under deep conviction. It was growing late, and our evangelist had to leave to tramp the miles back to the native inn where the band was staying.
>
> The next evening the mother and daughter of this family appeared over the high hills and mountains to reach the inn where we were staying. They planned to stay all night and get saved. Hour after hour we talked with them, and at one o'clock in the morning the light shone into their hearts. What a time of rejoicing they had. They insisted that the missionary come to their home the following night so that they could hear still more. This they agreed to do, and the master and the old grandfather, 89 years of age, were gloriously saved. The daughter gave her life wholly to the

> Lord and wants to start at once in our Bible school in Tokyo.
>
> These are some of the questions she asked: "Will I ever be able to come home to see my father and mother again? Will I be permitted to write them letters?" The vows that Buddhist nuns take when they enter temple service would require them to answer these questions in the negative. Yet, this precious girl was ready to go to all lengths for her new-found Lord Jesus. Think of these things, my dear friends, in our enlightened homelands when quibbling over some trifling "sacrifice" for the Lord!

That same month in the issue of *The Missionary Standard*, John Orkney reported:

> While in the Kagoshima city area, I noticed a single distant home on the side of a hill. I was tempted to think that no one lived there as it was small and looked very shabby. Then I felt checked and decided I must go. As I approached the house, just inside the door I saw a handsome lady, going about on her knees using a stick for a cane. I handed her a Gospel portion telling her it was the book of the true God. She smiled and reached out to accept the portion. I now saw that she was a leper, her fingers, as it were, eaten off. Only the stubs of the thumbs remained. As I left I felt as though my heart would break. I went away weeping and calling to God on her behalf. Who knows but what she is in the valley of decision and seeking after God since she has now learned of Jesus and His power to save.
>
> While working in Nagasaki city one day, it was rainy and cold so that I wore an overcoat. Quite a distance from the city, we came upon a home where just a few feet from the door of the home was a cage. In it was a young man of about 30 lying on the floor. He had gone insane. As we approached the cage, I asked my Japanese colleague about this pathetic scene. To my amazement the insane man,

hearing me speak in English, addressed me with these words, “A pound of butter, yes, yes. Thank you, thank you.” He then began to mutter words neither the native worker nor I could understand. My heart was wrenched by the scene and more so because it was on a cold, rainy day and he had only a thin kimono to wear.

My partner told the young man’s mother about Jesus and His power to save. It was clear her heart was deeply touched and she wept bitterly. She then told him that her son had been in that condition six years, and during that period of time she had wept for him every day. When I heard this I, too, was weeping, my eyes wet with tears. I cried to God on behalf of that poor mother. For six years she had bowed before her idols seeking deliverance for her boy, only to be met by dumb silence. But now she has heard of Jesus, and she perhaps, too, has decided to walk in the light. Pray for this dear family.

Chapter 12

THE BLIND MAN

Of the millions of Gospels and tracts that were distributed, very little is known as to the outcome of those sacred missiles. We will have to wait till we arrive safe on the other side to learn of the wonderful and unfathomable results of sowing the seed of the Word in human lives. Of all of the known results, perhaps the most incredible is the story which Paul Haines tells in his autobiography:

> It was about four o'clock one afternoon when we approached a young blind man who was perhaps about 16 years of age. We handed him the Gospel portion and booklet entitled "The Way of Peace." He was so shocked as to break out into an angry laugh, shouting, "What is this? What do you mean? Can't you tell that I'm blind? You expect me to read?" I responded, "Yes, I know you are blind, but this is the Word of God. Take it home with you and have someone read it to you." With this word, he accepted the booklet and thrusting it into his kimono sleeve proceeded punching his white cane in the gravel as he made his way down the road toward home.
>
> That same night just after having crawled under the heavy black mosquito net to retire on my tatami bed, I heard a noise at the door. I reached up to turn on the light and called "come in." Slowly the sliding door opened and the blind man entered bowing to the floor as he approached. "I wanted to make further inquiry about this book you gave me this afternoon," he said. A few mats on which to sit were quickly brought, and one of my fellow workers was called to assist in our conversation. The blind man said he had taken the Gospel and had someone read it to him. Now he had come to learn more about the way of salvation. In about 20 minutes, we had a new convert to Christianity. A

beam of light seemed to steal across his blind face as a smile broke out from ear to ear. He was now a new creature in Christ Jesus and in truth "the old things had passed away." After prayer and some instructions as to how to live a Christian life, we bade him good-bye and he returned home a happy soul.

We left the community the following day, hardly expecting to see him again. Some 13 years later, while I was serving as a missionary in Korea, I had occasion to return to Japan and visit that community again. By that time I had forgotten where I had met that blind brother. Our travels took us to the famous Aso volcano where we discovered that Bishop Nakada was conducting a revival. That night we attended the service. On seeing us, Bishop Nakada invited us to the pulpit to sit with him. As soon as I was seated, he leaned over and asked, "Do you see that blind man sitting near the post in the rear?" I replied that I did. Then the Bishop inquired, "Do you know who he is?" Oh, what joy. What a happy surprise to realize that this was the blind man I'd led to the Lord 13 years earlier.

After the service, we had a pleasant visit and then I bade him good-bye, returning to Korea the next day. Several years later, while sitting at my desk in the OMS headquarters in Los Angeles, I received a letter from Reverend E.L. (Bud) Kilbourne in Japan. He wrote, "We have a blind man named Reverend Yasuda out here who tells us that you led him to the Lord 35 years ago before the war. He has a Braille press and publishes a Christian newspaper for the blind." I was amazed, dumbfounded, felt like shouting "Hallelujah." Kilbourne went on to say: "During the war this press was destroyed, and he is wondering if I could help him get another. I took the news to Dr. B.H. Pearson of World Gospel Crusades and he responded, 'Why, surely. We will see that this brother gets that press' and it was done."

In 1957, while attending the 50th anniversary of our OMS Korea work, I stopped in Japan and our field leader, Dr. Roy Adams, took me down to Yokohama to visit with my blind friend. He asked us to join him for tea with the blind staff of his newspaper. Then he asked me to speak to them. This I did, recalling the miracle that happened so many years ago when I'd met a blind young man trudging along a county road near the volcano. Before I left, Reverend Yasuda said, "Brother Haines, last year the Lord enabled me to lead over 400 souls to Himself."

Later I learned that my blind friend was afflicted with tuberculosis. Then I received a message from him on tape. He said, "I am very weak, having only a few more days to live but I wanted one more time, before I go to heaven, to thank you for bringing the light of the Gospel to my soul." His voice then grew weaker as he bade me a last good-bye.

This is a story that I have repeated often but one day my son Meredith, who had taught for a time in Tokyo, said, "Dad, you left out a part of that story." "What did I leave out?" I asked. He replied, "Mister Yasuda, the blind man's son, was one of my students while teaching in the OMS Tokyo Bible seminary." I also omitted mentioning in the above comment on Reverend Yasuda's Braille Christian newspaper for the blind that it has made its way to all parts of Asia where Japanese blind are able to read the Braille—in Shanghai, Manchuria, Korea, Formosa, Hong Kong, South Sea Islands, and elsewhere.

A short time later I received a cable informing me that my dear blind brother, Reverend Yasuda, had entered the celestial city. I thought to myself not for one mile of the 5,000 or more which I walked in that village campaign could I have a tinge of regret when it produced a spiritual treasure like Reverend Yasuda. And it will continue to bear an even larger harvest of fruit. I have no doubt that there are many other "Yasudas" who we will one blessed day learn about.

Originally the plan was that The Great Village Campaign would be completed in 1917. Toward the end of the year, however, it became apparent that the task would likely take at least a month longer. For the GBS boys this would mean another month-long absence from school. OMS, however, felt certain that GBS would be happy to allow this extension in order to reach the last of the 10,400,000 homes. In *God's Revivalist* of January 1918 appears an article from the Cowmans entitled "The Ten Boys in Japan" and addressed to Sister Knapp.

> The time is rapidly approaching when the village work will be finished. These ten wonderful boys shall start home. I know you will be glad to see them, but I want to tell that we will be sorry to let them go for they have been a blessing all over the land and their true worth will only be known when Jesus comes.
>
> They have stood every test, and some of them have been severe for they have labored under all conditions and most of the time without proper interpreters. In addition, they have endured many petty difficulties that surely try one's faith and experience. But they have all stood true. Praise God!
>
> We had hoped they might return early in December so as to continue their school work, but it seems now that they will not finish the work until the end of January. We are certain the trustees and teachers of God's Bible School will help them to make up what studies they may miss by this extension. We trust that you will understand this delay and will do all you can for them as they are each one good boys and excellent workers . . . Please ask the whole school to continue praying for their classmates that they may be kept in health and strength to finish the work.

Chapter 13

"HALLELUJAH! THE WORK IS FINISHED!"

In the January 1918 issue of *The Missionary Standard*, there appears the following on the front page. In anticipation of the conclusion of The Great Village Campaign are large letters almost an inch tall, exclaiming "Hallelujah!" Then in smaller type, "The Japan Village Campaign is finished!"

Cowman writes:

> By the time this reaches our homeland, the great work of taking the Gospel to every home in Japan will have been completed, and we may have the time to stop and celebrate for the very momentum of its joy, its privileges and the newly revealed responsibilities and results. This puts us right over into the start of a similar campaign in needy and ripe Korea where already about 10,300 homes have been reached. Beloved fellow helpers, you have made this possible. Shout the victory with us! **Give Jesus All the Praise.**

In this same issue are the final reports from the young GBS evangelists who are here called "The Village Boys." Hal C. Hiles writes:

> "Fear thou not for I am with thee. Be not dismayed for I am Thy God. I will strengthen thee, yea, I will help thee. Yea, I will uphold thee with the right hand of my righteousness" (Isaiah 41:10). This scripture came to me shortly after arriving in Japan, as I asked the Lord for some proof of His seal upon my mission. Although I must confess, I was not as brave as I might have been that first night in a foreign land. When the Lord spoke to me in the above scripture, it was a real uplift. He meant more to me than money or military protection or even dear friends. It was our commanding captain speaking in words that no mortal could utter with

such tenderness and power. How often He has verified these words to me while in the Orient.

Those who have gone through such experiences have realized to some extent what it means to have God assure a person that he is pleased with his life and the course that he pursues in the face of misunderstandings (because of not having the language) and wickedness in various forms. God has led and enabled us to triumph.

He has enabled us to get the Gospel into many thousands of homes. God has confirmed our calling by sending us hungry souls who are seeking the true and living God. Each one is a proof that our work is not in vain.

We serve the true living God. Let us buckle on the armor and press forth into the battle with determination that the world shall not surpass us in accomplishments for our commander and leader. Souls are dying without the Gospel and how will we answer if we fail to do our part. We had better "wear out than to rust out." Certainly He will never fail us. If you have not already begun, begin today praising Him that you have an important part in this great work.

This was followed by a final report from William H. Miller:

"Oh, that my head were waters and my eyes a fountain of tears that I might weep day and night for the slaying of the daughter of my people" (Jeremiah 9:1). The prayer of Jeremiah has been my prayer since I came in contact with heathenism. My heart has wept ever since I first saw the spiritual state of the Japanese. When I think of the sacred command that was given to the Christian church 1900 years ago and how teeming multitudes of benighted souls are still waiting without the knowledge of the Gospel (100,000 going into eternity every 24 hours), I cry to the Holy Spirit that He would wake up the sleeping churches until they catch the vision that the weeping prophet had and that every Christian would look beyond friends, homeland and loved ones and say with Isaiah, "Here am I Lord, send me." I am willing to spend and be spent for the evangelization of the lost and fulfill the sacred command of our Savior.

I received a letter recently from a friend in America in which he stated, "I have just come from camp meeting but did not see any visible results." He further stated, "I think we should ship all our preachers to Japan where souls are dying without the knowledge of the Savior." Think of it, a camp meeting running 10 to 14 days without seeing anyone saved!

Beloved, if the Japanese had the chances the people in so-called Christian countries have, it would be no time until thousands would be born into the kingdom of God and the heart of Jesus would be made glad. Angels would rejoice, heaven populated, the devil defeated and hell robbed.

I have had as many as 50 seekers here in one street meeting. Recently we held a street meeting in a village of 600 houses. God put His seal on the service. Hearts were melted. The Holy Ghost was faithful and people stood in tears. The meeting closed. The invitation was given for all those who wanted Jesus to fill their hungry hearts to come to the native inn where we were stopping. Three young men followed us. The room in the inn was saturated with the presence of God, and it was not long before these young men were transformed from raw heathen to shining Christians.

The following day we were going to a village about 12 miles away. We started early as we had to distribute along the way. One of our workers testified to his friend how God had transported him from darkness and sin into His marvelous light and salvation. As they talked together, the man asked, "Where are the Christians? I want them to talk to me, to pray for me, to lead me into this blessed experience."

The next day this man in a kind of torment went to another friend and said, "Please come with me. I must find the Christians." They both got their bicycles and started about 2:30 p.m. to hunt for us. I had left the road and was going to visit some houses by a tile factory and was singing as I walked, "Oh, Thou in whose presence my soul takes delight." Then I heard someone calling. I looked around to see two men approaching on bicycles. I realized at once that one of them was in great trouble for I never saw a sadder countenance. I called my interpreter. The young man now cried, "I want to be saved. We have ridden all day looking for you." I suggested that we go up on the side of the hill and pray. We all knelt down under some pine trees and my interpreter read John 3:16, I John 1:9 and Jeremiah 29:13. There God wonderfully met with us.

So many of us who profess to love Christ live self-centered and self-indulgent lives. After we are saved and sanctified, we think that nothing more is required. Beloved, Jesus needs you to help evangelize the lost, the millions who have never once heard the Gospel.

The Great Village Campaign is completed in Japan. Before long, we will sing the doxology. In time we shall see the fruit from the seeds that have been sown with your prayers. God has promised, "My Word shall not return unto me void, but it shall accomplish that which I please and it shall prosper in the thing whereunto I sent it" (Isaiah 55:11).

The following letter from Everett Williamson appeared in the same issue:

Dear Brother Kilbourne, Praise God the victory is ours. We arrived at Ugy last night on a broken bicycle and two yen in our pockets but with lots of grace in our hearts and victory in our souls. Glad you had some money waiting for us.

We need to pray for some Buddy Robinsons out here. We need a "backbone like a sawed log and a wagon-load of determination stored up in the gable-end of our souls." In the homeland, we like to go by feeling, but here we must stand and fight the devil on the eternal truths of God's Word.

One day at Joge Machi where we were stationed, I started out in the morning weary just thinking of the hard day before us. The devil was attacking my soul with fiery darts. I prayed hard as I went along, and in a little while God drove him away. I finished the day feeling fine in soul and body. These hard places only make us more determined to fight on and lift up Jesus before those who are still in darkness. We can go to God for help every time Satan attacks us but these people are at the mercy of the enemy. They know not God.

A short time ago, while passing a temple up in a grove, I looked up and saw a woman praying. When I returned she was still there praying in great earnestness. My heart was moved with compassion. I climbed up the long flight of steps and spoke to her. I told her what I was doing and that I was a Christian. She said she had received one of our booklets that morning and was reading it but did not understand it. I found she was sick and had come to pray for healing, so there by that heathen temple I knelt and prayed for her. I asked that the light might come to her soul and that God would heal her body for His glory. When I began to pray, she was pounding her back in pain but as I prayed she stopped. I believe God was answering prayer and touching her body. I think of that dear woman often and wonder if she is still in darkness. She is only one of the millions that is sitting by the heathen temple waiting for you and me to bring them the light of life. God called Israel to be a light to the nations. When Jesus came, he commissioned the church to take the light of salvation to the nations. When he comes again, will he find the work finished?

Juji Nakada, far left, with Village Campaign evangelists

Cowmans on deputation

The new Village Campaign missionaries with the Cowmans and friends in Los Angeles

GBS boys farewelled en route to villages with Scripture packs – 1917

Everette Williamson at local wedding with Juji Nakada, first row right – 1917

Japan Holiness Church annual convention, Tokyo – 1926

Japan Holiness Church annual convention on Bible School compound – circa 1929

Japan Holiness Church Centennial Celebration 2001. Rev. Kuramada, seated center. Pastors holding photos of OMS founders (L to R): Charles Cowman, Tetsusaburo Sasao, Juji Nakada, E.A. Kilbourne

Graduating class of Seoul, Korea, Bible Training Institute - 1928

E.A. Kilbourne, OMS President - 1925

OMS Korea and China missionaries – 1940
Front Row: (kneeling) Harry Woods, Bud Kilbourne (standing) Ed Erny, Mary Woods
2nd Row: Paul Haines, Duncan McRoberts, Mildred Rice w/Kathleen, Robert Erny, Esther Erny, Emily Woods, John Woods, Lettie Cowman, Hazel Kilbourne, Rachel Woods, Myrtle Haines, unknown, Eunice Marais, Aletta Jacobsz, Maethorn and Lee Jeffries, Eugene Erny, Paul Haines, Jr.
Top row: Winnie McRoberts, Ida Tate, Rolland Rice, Edna Kunkle, Rosalind Rinker, Joy Woods

OMS Korea Bible School – circa 1930

Paul Haines with Rev. K. Yasuda. Shortly before his death in 1957.

Chapter 14

FAREWELL

In a farewell John Orkney wrote:

> I shall ever be thankful for the privilege of being in Japan to work for Jesus in The Great Village Campaign in the year 1917. It has blest my life in many ways. It has given me a little insight into the work of the missionary who must sacrifice, be strong and very courageous, and be patient in working with those in heathen darkness. God has been pleased to lead me in paths I did not expect. Still, He brought me through with a greater determination to be true to my Lord and to a lost world. Many things that I have experienced have been pleasant and a good many unpleasant. But praise God we need not fail if we keep our eyes on Jesus.
>
> In one town we had placed a Gospel portion in every home as well as in the surrounding villages. A few days later people thronged in to take part in a festival. A local pastor took advantage of the opportunity and sent a man out to sell Bibles. In one day he sold 11. At another place where we stopped, we met a young man whom a friend was seeking to lead to Christ. The boy received one of our Gospel portions which helped him to see clearly that Jesus is the Savior of the world. That night at a prayer meeting, he testified, "I see clearly now that Jesus is the Savior through reading a little book today entitled, 'The God You Should Worship'." Then and there he accepted Jesus Christ as his Savior. Praise God.
>
> In a country inn where we were staying, I noticed one of the servant girls had a very sad countenance, in fact, sadder than I'd ever seen before. Immediately, I felt a burden for her salvation, and I began to pray for her. That day we

placed the Gospel portion in the homes of the town. The next day on our return to the inn I noticed that same girl weeping. I suggested that my Japanese partner ask her if she had received sad news from home, but this was not the problem. He then told her of Jesus' love but she replied, "I believe in my god."

The next night after our evangelistic meeting, several stayed to be prayed for. The servant girl joined them, but she could not grasp the truth. The following day as we were leaving she bade us farewell, but her countenance was still sad. Please pray for her.

I have seen thousands of these poor souls going to their temples to pray and have watched them ring a bell to call the gods. I have seen them in the inns beseeching help from their idols but they, too, found no peace. Such are the conditions everywhere. Please pray much for the work that God may be glorified and many precious souls saved.

Harry Woods begins his testimony with this poem:

The sands have been washing in the footprints
Of the stranger on Galilee's shore
And the voice that subdued the rough billows
Is heard in Judea no more.
But the path of that lone Galilean
With joy I will follow today
And the toils of the road will seem nothing
When I get to the end of the way.

It's true, the waves have washed the footprints away and we do not behold the physical form of Jesus. However, He has left behind Him a path which the elements of nature have not been able to erase, one which every true saint has traveled as they have followed Him. This path is marked with toil, with suffering, and with loneliness in that He unceasingly, untiringly labors for the ministry of others; suffering in that His great heart felt the load under which the world was staggering, as well as the suffering of misunderstanding and of wounds received at the hands of men; loneliness in that He traveled the way alone.

At first glimpse of this way, one is greatly inclined to shrink but there is a great incentive—it is the end. It was the goal which prompted Christ to travel it. Isaiah says, “You shall see the travail of his soul and be satisfied.” Ah, what was the great incentive? It was a vision of a redeemed world.

The way is difficult to follow and cannot be walked merely in human strength. During my house to house visitation while pastor of a church in West Virginia, I remember seeing a motto which read “Teach me Lord Thy steps to trace, strong to follow in Thy grace.” Many times have I found occasion to pray this prayer since coming to Japan. How often has the way seemed hard and, at intervals, indiscernible. Still He taught me the right steps to take. Again there were seasons when my soul was tempted to shrink back. Then with the same wonderful grace that buoyed Him up during His life, He helped me to prevail and all the time He kept me singing, “Lord, I would clasp my hand in thine, nor ever murmur or repine, intent whatever lot I see since ‘tis God’s hand that leadeth me.”

It will only be a short time now before we can look at Japan and say that all of it has received the Gospel. Let us pray that the seed which has been shown may be mightily used of God in a harvest of souls. Amen.

The following are the valedictory words of Paul Haines:

I’m praising God this evening for that keeping power which is so valuable in a land like this where all is midnight, except the individual avenue which leads to the throne of grace. But even that, if we did not persevere, would close and become as it were a dome of steel because of the awful powers of darkness on every side. Again today I have been confronted by Japanese with the question, “What God is this? Where is this God?” We hear these questions no less than a dozen times every day and have to explain that our God is not a god of stone but lives and dwells in heaven.

The village work is a good place to learn to pray while you are on the move. I go to a house and find the family sleeping. I leave a tract and travel on my way, praying that when they wake up from their slumber they shall also awaken from their long slumber in sin. I go to another and find them threshing their rice and leave a tract, praying to the Lord to thresh sin out of their home. At another house I find them washing. I leave a portion with a prayer that their hearts may be washed in the precious blood and so forth. In each home, a tract, and in each home, a prayer. Oh dear ones, we are in a land where they read and where they write but where they actually have no sight.

The following entry is from Brother Thiele:

This is a city of many people in Japan. They have seen enough of religion, of bowing to gods of wood and stone, which neither give them peace nor satisfaction. Their hungry hearts are open to a knowledge of sins forgiven.

A few days ago we met a man who said, “I pray and sacrifice to my god but my religion has no force.” He knew that his prayers were not answered. Thank God some of these precious souls are finding Jesus. The village campaign is bringing Gospel truth and light which will point these hearts to the Lamb of God. Many are becoming discouraged with their religion and now is the time to give them the Gospel.

At one of the hotels where we were stopping, I noticed that the man occupying the room next to me would pray every morning, clapping his hands to get the attention of his god. This continued for days. One morning he came to us and asked how to know about Christianity. He had heard us pray, sing and praise the Lord and this, no doubt, caused him to inquire about our religion. How blessed to know that the Gospel of Christ "is the power of God unto salvation to everyone that believeth." I feel my soul mounting up as I give these booklets to the people. Thank God for the cleansing blood of Jesus that keeps me clean in the midst of awful sin. I rejoice to know Jesus as my personal Savior.

In Vernon Stanley's final report, he writes:

Dear Friends, I am glad that I can witness to victory through the blood of Jesus, my Savior. He is not only my Savior, but He is my keeper and my comforter. I am so glad that I tarried at the feet of Jesus and got my heart purged with the cleansing blood and the Pentecostal fire which came as a rushing mighty wind and killed the "old man." I am sure if he were not dead I would not be here today. I can say with Paul of old, "I am not ashamed of the Gospel of Christ for it is the power of God unto salvation to everyone that believeth."

I am so glad that "if the son of God makes a man free, he shall be free indeed." We should not be trying to hold unto some things belonging to the devil. I well remember before I was saved I was foolish enough to use some of the devil's trash and smoked many cigarettes though I tried to stop again and again. When I went down at the cross of Jesus to get saved, the devil came along and said, "You cannot stop smoking." I answered, "My Father can help me." There I prayed that the Lord would take the appetite away. Now for four years I have not wanted a cigarette. Not only that but He has taken away the desire for many other things. I am so glad that, if we will let Him, Jesus can make us truly free. I praise God and will glorify His name forever.

Not only is God able to make a man free but He can take away fear. Brother, just think about it, what a wonderful God we have. So many people say, "I fear I cannot stop." Bless God forever. He says, "Perfect love casts out fear." What is perfect love? Fire and the Holy Ghost. So many of our friends are lacking both the fire and the Holy Ghost. That is the reason there are so many poor souls in this land today who don't know about the precious blood of Jesus Christ that saves from sin. Oh God, help us to wake up to the fact that Jesus meant what He said when He spoke Mark 16:15: "Go into all the world and preach the Gospel to every creature." Well, you say, "I cannot go." Read Romans 10:14-15.

We just closed the meeting here and found that a church without the Holy Ghost will not lead souls to Christ. The place where we were was cold, no life and nobody would come to the meeting. The devil came up and said, "You won't do any good here." Then we went to God in prayer and told the Lord that we were His and we were here for Him. We rented a church and the first night we had about 20 people and 6 seekers. We kept on praying telling the Lord that people wanted Him, and we needed His help. We put up circulars all over the village advertising the meetings. On Sunday night we had about 100 people in the little church and others outside listening. We had 20 seekers, 5 of whom were brightly saved from sin. In all, we had 37 seekers and 12 who prayed through to victory. How we praise God that hell was robbed, the hearts of the angels made to rejoice, and our souls blessed. Praise God forever. We give Him all the glory for He has done great things! Please pray that all who heard about Jesus will seek until they find peace at the foot of the cross.

> As the village work will be completed by the time you receive this, we ask you to pray that God will give us a safe trip back to our homes. We truly want to be firebrands for God and warm up the hearts of our friends that they will do more than ever for these poor souls.

At the end of January 1918, most of the boys returned to God's Bible School to continue their education. Paul Haines and Harry Woods, however, agreed to stay on for a time. Although Japan proper had been covered in The Great Village Campaign, there remained two larger outlying islands, Formosa and Okinawa, both Japanese possessions. Although mission work in Formosa (now Taiwan) had been begun by the Presbyterian Church in the late 1800s, Okinawa was still for the most part totally untouched by the Gospel. Cowman and Kilbourne now agreed to continue the campaign until every home in Okinawa (then called LooChoo) had been reached as well. Harry Woods volunteered to assist in the completion of the campaign. In the May issue of *The Standard* is the article entitled, "Advance in LooChoo Islands."

The *God's Revivalist* summary of The Great Village Campaign continues:

> The distribution work in the southern islands was accompanied by refreshing showers sent from the Father above as you will note from the several accounts of that work in this issue. We have discovered, as it were, a great harvest field ready for the reapers which presents a tremendous call for workers. We must do something for those island souls. Apart from the worship of the dead spirits and their ancestors at the tombs, these people have no system of religious worship, although Buddhism is arriving among them now, along with the Japanese immigrants. All our village campaign workers are impressed with the present, ripe opportunity in LooChoo. We feel we must hasten to buy up the opportunity.

> We plan to open a mission hall in the capital city of Naha. This will also serve as the headquarters for a district superintendent. We must have a pastor and assistant for street work and general evangelistic effort. Then we will open at least two other centers.

In the same issue, Harry Woods under the title, "The Solitary Place Shall Be Glad," writes:

> Can you imagine a nation whose cities have been razed to the ground and have been robbed of its people; whose fertile fields once known for their fruitfulness have become a parched and thirsty ground, a burning sandy desert, the sole habitation of dragons, reptiles and scorpions; whose verdant trees have been divested of their once beautiful foliage and become a waste, howling wilderness?
>
> And again can you imagine a land without a church or a Bible preacher or Christian whose people are bowing down to the spirits of their ancestors or to gods of wood and stone; bound by the fetters or superstition; engrossed in the most intense darkness; looking into a blank and hopeless future, wondering what is beyond? There is not a one of you who would desire to live in such a place. Even an avowed atheist was known to say, "If all the churches and every Christian influence were removed from my community, I would not wish to live there!" Yet, throughout the breadth of the earth are many such places as the one described above. One of these in particular I will bring before your vision—Yaeyama and Miyako counties, a part of Okinawa. These two counties comprise three large islands and eight small ones and a population of about 75,000 people. The sad part of it is they have neither a church nor a preacher. We have yet withheld from them the "bread of life." Now we are determined to place the Gospel in every home, and we are praying that the printed Word may be an instrument in the salvation of their souls. In fact, we are already seeing results. Everywhere we go to hold

street meetings hundreds of people come and some have believed in Jesus while others expressed a desire to know more about Him.

Then can you fancy these cities being rebuilt to a grandeur and beauty far exceeding anything known in the past; of their being inhabited by a people separated for years from their native land who have looked forward with longing and anticipation to the time when they should return? Then can you see that desert blossoming as the rose; that parched and thirsty land becoming a pool of water with streams breaking forth from the wilderness?

Ah, Friends, these people are ripe for the Gospel. In all my Christian experience, I have never seen anything like it. The saddest part about it is that we had to leave the newly-born babes in Christ as lambs without a shepherd. However, we are planning to send them a preacher soon and also establish a church. The foundation of God's Word and a Savior has been laid and, by the help of God, we are expecting to see rise a noble band of saints who will constitute a part of Christ's body and meet Him when He comes.

When you read these lines, can you wonder that I quote Isaiah's words, "The solitary place is glad"? Won't you take Yaeyama and Miyako on your hearts, praying that we shall be enabled soon to send them a preacher and build them a church.

Tell it again, tell it again
Salvation's story repeat, o'er and o'er
Till none shall say of the children of men
Nobody ever has told me before.

Chapter 15

"YES, AGAIN YES!"

With most of the GBS boys back on the campus, Ernest Kilbourne no doubt felt a need for an official summing up of The Great Village Campaign. In the March 1918 issue of *The Missionary Standard* are headlines reading: **"Again? Yes, Again and Again!"**

> We would bring to your minds by way of remembrance the vital importance of importunate prayer for this great seed-sown empire.
>
> **The Results** which have accompanied and followed The Great Village Campaign have set our hearts aflame. Now, we see the prospect of the wondrous harvest that can be reaped by a prayer-saturated special tent campaign over the ground that has been so thoroughly covered in this seed sowing.
>
> **Taps**: We challenge you to pray for every home in Japan touched by the campaign. The mighty effort part is ours; the prevailing prayer part is yours as well as ours. We are now launching a tent campaign to cover the empire. We plan to hold several days of meetings in the larger centers where we can gather those who have received the Gospel portions and seen the gleaming of a great light.

Nearly a century has passed since the completion of The Great Village Campaign in Japan and Okinawa and the return of the "splendid boys" to the homeland. All but two of them completed their training at God's Bible School. Very little is known of most of those young heroes in later life. However, in the centennial publication of God's Bible School entitled, "God's Clock Keeps Perfect Time," are the following brief resumes:

Lewis Hiles: Lewis, later, was a Pilgrim Holiness missionary to the West Indies. He died November 4, 1973.

John Orkney: When Orkney returned to the campus at age 25, he married Anna May Neff, sister to Paul Haines' wife, Myrtle. The two couples then worked together in Korea. The Orkneys later returned to the States to pastor in Oregon.

Rollie Poe: Rollie graduated from God's Bible School at age 25. After the campaign, he became a United Methodist pastor. He died in 1968.

William Miller: William completed his education at God's Bible School in 1919. He then returned to the Orient with his wife. They worked in Korea under The Oriental Missionary Society until 1922, after which they returned to the U.S. where William became a Nazarene evangelist.

Vernie B. Stanley: Vernie completed his schooling at God's Bible School. We know nothing of his activities in later life.

Everett Williamson: After completing his schooling at God's Bible School, Everett and his wife went to Japan for six years as missionaries with the Evangelical United Brethren church. They returned to the States in 1930. Their son, Lowell, was part of the second Every Creature Crusade in the 1950s. He spent two years in Japan and six months in Taiwan. Like his father, he was part of a campaign to put the Scriptures in every home and also to organize churches. He later graduated from Asbury College and Western Evangelical Seminary and married Naomi Bletscher. They returned to Taiwan with OMS where Lowell was field leader for many years. His son, Rodney, also joined OMS and presently serves as Taiwan field director.

Paul Haines: Following the campaign in Japan, Paul married Myrtle Neff, and they went to Korea to work with OMS. He eventually became director of the work there. After World War II, they returned to Korea for a time and then located in Los Angeles where Paul served as OMS treasurer as well as southeast regional director. He died in 1976. Both of their sons, Paul and Meredith, served on OMS mission fields.

Edward Oney: Edward worked in The Great Village Campaign beginning in 1914. Cowman sent him back to the U.S. in 1916 to recruit others. After graduation from GBS, Edward became an effective church planter for the Nazarenes, particularly in West Virginia.

William Thiele: William graduated from GBS and with his new wife he returned to the Orient (Korea) with the Millers and Orkneys in 1919. He later pastored Nazarene churches in the United States.

Harry Woods: Harry remained in the Orient after the other members of the GBS team returned home in 1918. He first helped evangelize the island of Okinawa and later assisted OMS work in Korea. He served in OMS for 47 years in Korea, China, Taiwan, and Brazil. In both China and Taiwan, he was appointed field director. Harry and his wife, Emily, were the last OMS missionaries to leave China after the Communist takeover. Their son John, with his wife, Janet, also served for a time with OMS as a missionary doctor in Ecuador.

OMS commenced missionary work in Korea in 1913. As in Japan, their first objective was to establish evangelistic centers and Bible schools to train pastors, evangelists and Bible women.

The news of The Great Village Campaign also spread to Korea and inspired a similar program there. Ernest Kilbourne and John Thomas are credited with establishing an OMS beachhead in Seoul and building the first OMS Bible Institute, a large four-storey structure, at this time the highest building in the city. John and Mary Thomas from Great Britain were the first missionaries in residence and appointed field directors. Sadly, they were forced to retire from the field after a savage and near-fatal beating that almost took John's life. Thereafter, they served the mission in the U.S., locating in Wilmore, Kentucky.

A great revival in Korea during the early years of the 20th century laid the foundation for some of the largest churches in the world. This also precipitated a great missionary movement. Today Korea sends abroad more missionaries per capita than even the United States. The OMS Holiness Church was a part of this great drama and is today the third largest denomination in Korea with more than 2,000 churches and a membership exceeding 1,000,000.

The Great Village Campaign in Korea never enjoyed the same success as Japan. This is largely due to the fact that though some Koreans were learning to read Japanese, as well as their own mother tongue, for the most part the nation was illiterate. The people never developed the passion for reading that characterizes the Japanese. Hence, the effectiveness of using printed scripture and Gospel tracts was greatly reduced. In addition, the Korea village campaign was interrupted by World War II, and every home in the nation was never reached with Scriptures as in Japan.

When OMS opened work in China in 1921, they again instituted a Great Village Campaign for that nation. Later this effort, now renamed the Every Creature Crusade, was carried on in other fields, including India, Colombia, Brazil, and Ecuador. It is significant that during the second half of the 20th century the OMS program to reach every home became the inspiration for other organizations that to this day are making similar efforts throughout the world. The best known of these is probably Every Home Crusades.

Although in 1918 The Oriental Missionary Society completed a task which no other agency or church had ever before accomplished, this feat was not without its critics.

It was common for church and mission agencies to voice their opinion that so superficial a scattering of the Gospel seed would be unlikely to produce any enduring harvest. And without a doubt as in Christ's parable, much of the seed would be "devoured by birds." Some reported that the tracts were appreciated mainly because they made ideal cigarette wrapping and were also excellent for starting fires. Others averred that most of the Gospel tracts "fell among thorns" or upon dry, unreceptive or stony soil. The entire exercise, they judged, was an expensive waste of time unworthy of the cost and sacrifice involved. Some admitted that OMS' quixotic endeavor was likely to have some residual benefit, although for the most part it was little more than a kind of publicity stunt designed to attract attention, raise money or recruit workers.

Some suggested that Cowman and Kilbourne, though sincere brothers, but without the benefits of secondary education, had been hoodwinked and their good intentions, not withstanding, could not expect any great or enduring fruit for their efforts.

Others, however, pointed out that the fervor of the American boys with their naïve assumption that they were evangelizing Japan was the very kind of mustard-seed faith that God has promised to bless.

The facts are these. During and after The Great Village Campaign, OMS converts wonderfully multiplied; churches were crowded; and young Christians thronged into the mission's already crowded schools, producing graduates with the same heady conviction that Gospel tracts and scripture were effectively impacting the hearts of their fellow countrymen.

By 1930 OMS had planted hundreds of churches in Japan. Their annual conferences attracted an attendance of several thousand. Moreover the OMS Japan Holiness Church had soared to a position as the third largest Protestant denomination in Japan, so large in fact that OMS began locating most of their new missionaries in other fields, especially Korea and China.

The original vision of The Oriental Missionary Society fulfilled in part Ernest Kilbourne's dream. In this vision, en route to Japan, he saw a great bridge arching across the Pacific. The first span stretched from the U.S. to Japan; the second from Japan to China; and the third from China to India. This encompassed most of Asia—the greatest block of human beings on earth. Later Lettie Cowman had a similar vision: The Every Creature Crusade born in the Orient was to extend to Europe, South America and other continents. After all, had not Christ's command been to take the Gospel to every creature?

Chapter 16

THE TERRIBLE TOLL

Towards the end of The Great Village Campaign in Japan in1918, Charles and Lettie's strenuous life style began more and more to exact a terrible toll. For 17 successive years, they had voyaged to the U.S. and back for the purpose of visiting hundreds of churches, colleges and camp meetings. Here they reported on the OMS endeavor, particularly The Great Village Campaign, and solicited both prayer and financial support. All of this constituted an increasingly unreasonable burden. Such was the great cost of implementing the vision of placing the Word of God in every Japanese home. It was this inhuman labor that Lettie often said cost Charles his life, making her husband a martyr and herself, a widow.

In fact, Lettie had begun experiencing her own heart problems as early as 1914. Then in 1917 Charles, after hours in prayer, confided to Lettie that he was being troubled by heart pains. He knew he should rest, slow down, and take a sabbatical. Yet, though he feared he might be dying, he told her he could "find no stopping place." The work must go on. The task must be completed. Later Lettie often said, "The vision cost him his life."

That year during deputation travels in the state of Michigan, Charles collapsed. "Your work is at an end," the doctor told him. "If you are to survive, you must stop and take long-term bed rest." The Cowmans made it back to Los Angeles, but there Charles entered the first stage of invalidism.

Charles' long and terrible siege of sickness and weakness now rendered it impossible for either him or Lettie to undertake OMS responsibilities apart from some correspondence. Although Charles remained titular head of the mission, it was largely his beloved partner, Ernest Kilbourne, who carried the executive responsibilities.

Charles' great trial by cardiac torment continued six years. A series of healing meetings and anointings, for a brief time, seemed to help but eventually the old pain returned, more torturous than ever. In the process, Lettie was battling for her faith. Struggling with her own cardiac problems, she remained a constant nurse to Charles. To survive this dark, seemingly interminable trial, she began to gather poems and devotional readings from magazines on the theme of sorrow and suffering. These she edited and sent to God's Bible School for regular publication in the school magazine. They later formed the substance of her incomparable devotional, *Streams in the Desert.*

Lettie now found special consolation in Exodus, chapter 14. Here is the record of the recently emancipated nation of Israel. Leaving Egypt they had come to the banks of the Red Sea. In front of them are fearful, rolling tides and behind the approaching armies of Egypt bent on re-enslaving the Hebrew nation. In Exodus, chapter 14 in Lettie's Bible, now a treasure in the mission's archives, one finds the pages stained with tears and rendered nearly illegible from constant reading.

The last two years of his life Charles was in such great pain he could not lie down for any length of time. Day and night he assumed a sitting posture. Without drugs, particularly morphine, he found it impossible to sleep or get relief. Toward the end as Lettie lay prostrate before her open Bible, verse 7 from John, chapter 13, was suddenly illuminated as by a heavenly light. She read Jesus' words to Peter at the last supper, "What I do thou knowest not now but thou shalt know hereafter." Before Lettie's eyes these words glowed with uncanny illumination. Yes, that was it. In that instant, she understood God's mysterious ways. Charles would not be healed in the way that humans usually demand. He would die. But from that death would burst forth something too glorious to comprehend. Did not Jesus himself, when approaching the shadow of the cross, cry, "Except a corn of wheat fall into the ground and die, it abideth alone; but if it die, it bringeth forth much fruit" (John 12:24)?

Charles died in September 1924 and was buried in the Hollywood cemetery. Now, for Lettie, there were weeks, even months, of paralyzing grief when she sat alone almost every afternoon beside the grave of her beloved. For a time the bright promises of God had seemed to be extinguished by the dark despair and confusion of these days. At times she now felt as though God had indeed deserted her. Her heart was so weak that doctors said that she could never again travel.

Then into this stygian darkness shone a glimmer of light. Her collected readings, most of which had been printed in *God's Revivalist* elicited increasing comment. She felt impressed to compile a daily devotional book which she would call *Streams in the Desert*. The printer calculated that 500 copies would be more than enough to meet any demand.

Some of the readers were not impressed. One, in an unpleasant temper, demanded her 25 cents back, saying the book was simply not worth that much money! Many, however, found that *Streams* had a divine, almost mystic, power and ineffable sweetness. It ministered to their suffering as no other book, other than the Bible. From the outset the growing demand for this amazing book has continued virtually without interruption. Millions of copies of *Streams in the Desert* have been and continue to be printed, and the book can be found in almost every American bookstore. Editions in many foreign languages have followed. Today, *Streams* ranks, along with *Pilgrim's Progress,* as one of the 20 most widely published books in the English language.

Although Ernest Kilbourne assumed the presidency of OMS upon the death of Charles, he survived his dear friend and compatriot by a mere four years. Immediately the board elected Lettie as mission president. There was no other possible choice.

OMS was now entering China but had apparently chosen a most inopportune time. The 1920s mark a period of violent uprisings by war lords in opposition to Chiang Kai-shek's attempt to unify all of

China under the nationalist government. So unsettled and dangerous was this time, particularly in Shanghai, that OMS missionaries for the most part relocated in Korea.

As Lettie Cowman's name became known, there followed a constant stream of invitations to speak in prominent churches and schools, as well as conventions and retreats. Sometimes, despite her weak heart, she would speak as many as three times a day and afterwards spend hours with inquirers and *Streams'* readers who, like herself, were experiencing a morass of helplessness and despair.

Chapter 17

THE BALTIC CRUSADE

(For this account of the Baltic Crusade, I am greatly indebted to Dr. Ben Pearson and his narrative in *The Vision Lives.*)

In his book *The Vision Lives,* B. H. Pearson writes:

> From Moody Bible Church there came more calls for messages from the aging missionary; Lettie recklessly accepts. She knows she is in God's hands. Now for each labor she discovers a new fund of energy. God is giving her healing. Symptoms of the weak heart and diminishing energy seem to disappear. Doctors examine her and declare that she has been healed. She plays and sings. One of her favorites is "He giveth more grace when the burdens grow greater; He giveth more strength as the labors increase; To added affliction He addeth his blessing; To multiplied sorrow His multiplied peace."

In all of this Lettie has not forgotten the vision of the Every Creature Crusade. In a century engulfed by the greatest wars in human history, she envisions white-knighted warriors, their tunics emblazoned with crosses, gladly accepting terrible risks to liberate foreign lands for Jesus. In 1936 with Japan preparing to invade China, Lettie received a cable from Swansea, Wales, inviting her to speak at an Every Creature Convention. Despite the strenuous journey and her increasing age, she felt led to accept. She gets a clear command from Scripture. And then a scrap of a poem: "This hour a grander work awaits your hand than any written in the treasured past; lay to the oar, the tide runs fast; life's possibilities are as yet unspanned."

Soon she boarded the plane for New York and then takes a ship for England. She seemed to hear divine instructions. "Let us pass on to the other side." The Atlantic crossing is routine. Arriving in

England, she was met by the Reverend Reese Howells (whose life story would later appear in the classic *Reese Howells, Intercessor*). He escorted her to Swansea Bible College.

Missionaries from many parts were present at the convention. After Lettie spoke Friday night, Howells insisted that she speak every night for the entire week. She proceeded to tell the story of Charles' vision for the Japan village campaign and its fulfillment. Now her heart was asking, "What next, Lord?" She felt certain she had come to Swansea in the will of God. After the convention, Reese Howells suggested, "Remain in your room. We will send meals to you. God has something to tell you."

At 6 a.m. on Sunday, August 10, 1936, the Lord spoke to her from Jeremiah, chapter one: "Then the word of the Lord came unto me saying, before I formed you in the belly, I knew thee; and before thou camest forth out of the womb, I sanctified thee and I ordained thee a prophet unto the nations." Sunday morning in a public service, she acknowledged that she has been called to something new. "From this hour on," she said, "I had a new commission."

The following day as she came out of the afternoon service, she met Anna Liisa and Sanfrid Mattsson, who had just arrived from Finland. They had heard of the Swansea Conference and read of the OMS crusade work in Japan. Now they had determined to put the Word into every home in Finland. The two million people of that little country were now added to Lettie's crusade vision. For three glorious hours she met with the Mattssons as they told her of their call. Finally she agreed to return to Finland with them. They immediately proceeded to book her passage on a cargo ship, the Kadir. Since there were no available state rooms, the captain offered to give her his cabin. That evening Lettie sat down at the piano, played and sang: "How sweet the thought that comes to me on mountain or on stormy sea. There is no land, nor clime, nor zone where Jesus leaves His sheep alone."

Quite unexpectedly twenty English pounds came in, then a check for ten pounds. Miss Crossley, a dear personal friend and heiress to

Frank Crossley's fortune, gave her 200 pounds for China. Three wool suits came in for the Finland trip. Miss Crossley loaned her fur coat to Lettie. God clearly was providing.

Wednesday, September 23, 1936, arrived. This was the day she had been scheduled to take the steamship Normandy for the United States. Now, instead, she found herself being conveyed 40 miles from Swansea to Cardiff, Wales. There she boarded the S.S. Kadir and was placed in the captain's cabin, better and more commodious than the cabin of a large liner. She was surprised that the fare was only 22 shillings. They sailed at 11 a.m. on September 24. The next day was the anniversary of Charles' homegoing.

Despite the rough North Sea, she loves it. She has always enjoyed a sense of adventure and writes, "My soul is filled with joy." Through the night the storm worsened as mounting swells tossed the ship about like a cork. All are sick, even the dear Estonian cook who valiantly struggled to serve faithfully the three passengers. Mrs. Cowman embraced her with a comforting hug and kiss. In her cabin as the violence increased, Lettie again read the first chapter of Jeremiah.

Approaching the Gulf of Bothnia near Finland, the sky, wind and sea unite in a fearful turmoil of seething and roiling waves. Strangely, in it all, Lettie seems to hear the deep thunderous tones of a great organ playing. At midnight when none could sleep, she sang, "Oh, how I love Him, how I adore Him, my breath, my sunshine, my all in all. The great creator became my Savior and all God's fullness dwelleth in Him."

Then the full terror of the storm struck. The ship's radio received numerous SOS messages. For three days and nights, the captain and helmsman do not leave the bridge, struggling on, utterly exhausted. Old hands say they have never seen such a sea. Many ships flounder and go down with the cargo, crew and passengers. Others are dashed to pieces against the rocks and cliffs. Lettie has a radio message sent to Swansea College: "Storm. Ship in danger. Pray." A request for prayer is also telegraphed to Jakodstad,

Finland, where friends have gathered to receive the Mattssons and Lettie.

In the midst of the storm, Lettie testified that God had given her perfect peace. Through that night she said her Father gathered her in His great arms and whispered, "Be not afraid." And still the sea raged on. The Estonian helmsman was in despair. The cook felt that she and all aboard would be lost. Finally, after the unspeakable tempest had spent itself, the sun appeared. Lettie's response was, "What a marvelous experience! I would not have missed it for the world." With prayers of gratitude they proceed on their way.

The disastrous hurricane over, she and the Mattssons commenced crusade plans for Lapland and Estonia, as well as Finland—three nations. She is enveloped in a wondrous calm that brings with it the sweet assurance that she is in the center of God's will.

At midnight the Kadir approached the harbor and a Finnish pilot came aboard. The storm had lengthened the voyage to 14 days. A small vessel came alongside. Mrs. Cowman and her fellow passengers clamored down the side of the ship on a rope ladder. The harbor is a scene of wreckage. The storm has swept away the floats and dislodged the stairway up the wharf. Despite the danger, she is forced to go it alone. With the stairs gone, she must climb the unsteady rope ladder to the top of the pier. She is in Finland

At 8 p.m. the Mattssons and Lettie take a train to Jakodstad. There at the platform she found a group of believers ready to welcome them. For six days these Finnish Christians had been waiting and watching in prayer. The next evening a missionary meeting was held in the local church. The place was crowded and there was an air of expectancy. Breathlessly the people listened as Lettie told them of the Japan crusade. This was followed by her passionate vision for a new campaign, this one in the Baltic States. The interpreter catches fire. Lives are challenged. Crusaders are enlisted. The miracle is repeating itself.

In an article for publication in America, Lettie shares her call to the nations. After 35 fruitful years in the Orient, now the borders are being enlarged. God has given her a fresh call; Charles' vision is a precursor to a new and deeper call. A great map of Finland and the Balkans is found and fastened prominently to the wall. Then hour by hour plans for a systematic distribution campaign are devised. In the process it seems to her that she and Charles are together again. It is agreed that Finland will be their first target. Next, workers will carry large packets of scriptures to Lapland. They will travel by sleds or skis over the icy mountains. Estonia's two million will get the Word. The next day they travel 300 miles along the Russian border.

At last the plan for the evangelization of Finland, Lapland and Estonia is completed. But how much will it cost? They add up the figures—$10,000—but they are not daunted. God has led. God will supply. His storehouse is full. She quotes, "The silver is mine and the gold is mine, saith the Lord of hosts." And then the words of Hudson Taylor, "God's man in God's work done in God's way will never lack God's supply."

From Finland Lettie and a band of crusaders leave for Lapland and cover the small country. They have allotted eight days to organize the campaign. They use various modes of transportation—train, auto and sleds—to convey them over land and through woodlands to the Artic Sea. Her heart is thrilled with the rugged beauty, the dense inviting forests. Some members of their team are flying over the snow on skis. With the gaiety of a child, Lettie enjoys the story-book experience of travel in reindeer-drawn sleds. Housing in these areas is primitive. As they entered arched huts in isolated places, they feel the loneliness of the Laplander's life.

Meetings were held everywhere. The school houses were packed as reindeer arrived, pulling well-filled sleds through blinding snowstorms. She had never known such sharp, bitter cold but how warm were the hearts of the people. More and more Christian men and women, she felt, were catching the vision. Heroic evangelists set out traveling hundreds of miles over the steep snow to reach lone Laplanders with the Word. One of the young workers traveled more than 500 miles on his skis, carrying a heavy pack of scripture portions on his back. He counted it a privilege and delight to endure the fatigue and the bitter cold for the cause of Christ. On one leg of the journey, Lettie was accompanied by a young Finnish brother. Though shy and reserved, he was a wonderful pianist and enrolled in a Bible college. He felt impressed to work among the Jews. Another of her companions was called to be a missionary to China.

The crusade's next target is Estonia. Here again, the people opened wide their arms to Lettie Cowman. As she spoke of Charles' vision, the Estonians wept. Never, it seemed, had she seen such joy-lit faces. The glorious work is begun. Evangelists volunteer to go from home to home with the Word of God. Elderly men and women with tears streaming down their faces grasp her hand in theirs and kiss it. They tell her, "You have come to bring Jesus to us." She becomes theirs. Her heart is again enlarged to take in Estonia. There are 100,000 copies of John's Gospel ordered in Estonian.

She learned that along the borders of Estonia were 80,000 Russians who had fled from the horrors of Stalinism. Some of them had been exiled and driven out. Hundreds more had starved to death. Whole villages were deserted without a single resident.

The Russians crowded their way into the small hall where she spoke. The message of love stirred their hearts, bringing tears to her eyes. As they left they began singing Charles' favorite hymn: "It may be at morn when day is awakening when Jesus receives His own." This is a scene she will never forget. Some take her hand and kiss it, urging her to come back and live among them.

In one of her meetings, a Russian lady was deeply moved. She felt led to go to the Russian border in Estonia and buy a stone house. The large front room served as a Gospel hall. A converted Communist and a young man from Finland volunteer to join Lettie. Now she is invited to speak in the Finnish parliament house where she meets a Finn who is paying for the support of two young evangelists for the whole winter. They will carry on the crusade.

A call now comes from Stockholm, Sweden's capital, where she is invited to a church that seats 4,000 people. That entire evening she told the story of Charles' vision of reaching the nations with the Word. The people are deeply moved. "Do they realize," Lettie thought, "what it cost the Son of God to redeem lost men—Laplanders, Estonians, Arabs, Egyptians, Chinese?"

There now followed crusade beginnings in Latvia, Poland, Rumania, and in the heart of Czechoslovakia. The efforts are soon deterred, however, for want of Gospel portions. She decides that she must hurry back to London to appeal for help from the Bible societies. Orders were placed for thousands of scriptures for the countries she had visited. When she returned to Scotland and England, a Baltic States' Bible Society was formed. They asked Lettie to take care of the correspondence and manage the business until the necessary committees can be organized.

Chapter 18

MEETING THE EMPEROR

While in London Lettie was invited to visit Haile Selassie, Emperor of Ethiopia. Mussolini, in a boast of restoring the Roman Empire, had overrun Ethiopia. Selassie had sought sanctuary in England until such a time as his throne could be recovered. Mrs. Cowman and her friends were escorted to the estate where the Emperor was residing. Two Ethiopian servants showed her to a waiting room and then into the presence of the Emperor. Lettie entered in silence, standing respectfully in Selassie's presence. The Emperor, a Coptic Christian, was thought to be a descendant of King Solomon and the Queen of Sheba. One of his several titles was Lion of the Tribe of Judah. Mrs. Cowman's message for the Emperor had been given her the night before: "For a small moment I have forsaken thee but with great mercies I will gather thee. In a little wrath, I hid my face from thee for a moment but with everlasting kindness I have mercy on thee, saith the Lord, thy redeemer" (Isaiah 54:7-8).

After delivering the message, Mrs. Cowman greeted and shook hands with each member of the royal household. The Queen offered Mrs. Cowman her arm and the two walked together into the dining room. The Emperor followed, escorted by the family. Lettie was seated at the Emperor's right and next to her one of the princesses. The servants were all Ethiopians. This made her feel like a member of the family, and all hearts were ready to receive her message. As she spoke of Calvary, they listened almost spellbound.

Of the entire family, the Emperor was the most attentive to his guest. He gently instructed them not to neglect her. Mrs. Cowman felt that he seemed more like a brother than a great ruler. Certainly the presence of the Lord Jesus Christ was in their midst, and she had come by divine appointment.

Seated by the Emperor's side, she felt as though she was on a throne. She told the story of *Streams in the Desert*, how it was birthed during Charles' illness, when she hungrily gathered words of comfort, words which in time became her beloved devotional book. At this the Emperor responded, "My people in Ethiopia are broken hearted. They need divine comfort. Could not this book minister to them? May I translate it for them?" Here the young princess spoke up, "Father, I will translate it." And thus *Streams* would be going forth in yet another language. Mrs. Cowman's cup of joy is full.

His majesty then showed Mrs. Cowman a large manuscript—a Bible inscribed on parchment bound in heavy brown leather. "For years," Selassie explained, "the best scholars of the nation have been working on this translation of the entire Bible into modern Ethiopian." Then, sorrowfully, he told of the cost of this translation. "Every one of the university-trained translators of the Ethiopian Bible was killed during Mussolini's war of conquest. I wonder if their blood is not crying out to God, 'How long, how long?'" At that point, Mrs. Cowman called for an English Bible and read Isaiah 54, explaining its significance to the Emperor.

They returned to the reception room where the family was waiting. Mrs. Cowman now felt impressed to say, "Let us talk to our heavenly Father." She then led in prayer. Never in her lifetime had she so sensed the presence of the Lord Jesus. At the close of the prayer, all stood in silence for what seemed like at least five minutes. There were tears in all their eyes. Then the Emperor said, "Will you not come with me to my little church?" He and the family then led her through the lovely English garden. The Emperor pointed to a bower surrounded by flowers. "This is the place I call my church," he said. Above the flowers was a cross and below a few benches. Upon the pulpit was a huge Bible written in Geeez, Ethiopia's ancient, now dead, language.

As Lettie prepared to leave, his majesty said, "Come into the house with me. Do not go just yet." When they were again inside, he presented Mrs. Cowman with a beautiful ring made of heavy

Ethiopian gold known as the gold of Ophir. “I want you to know,” he said, “that you are the only person since I have been in England who has ever come to me to speak of the Lord Jesus Christ. We have deeply appreciated it. Won’t you come again to us? Won’t you always come?”

That day a friendship was formed between Lettie and the Emperor. After the war when Selassie visited Los Angeles, he asked to be escorted to Lettie’s home on Hobart Boulevard. There then followed an unforgettable meeting so significant that is was even noted in the *Los Angeles Times.*

The Baltic crusades took on new significance in the months that followed. Soon all of Europe is engulfed in war. Then with the attack on Pearl Harbor the OMS’ fields in Japan, Korea, China, and Hong Kong are in Japanese hands. OMS missionaries in China are interned in prisoner of war camps and those in India advised to prepare to evacuate at a moment’s notice. Now, during these years of conflict and turmoil, the worst war in human history, what of Charles Cowman’s vision of taking God’s Word to every home in a nation?

OMS Korea Great Village Campaign team

OMS Peking Bible School – 1936

OMS China missionaries, Shanghai, 1937. In front: Woods' children - Rachel, Joy, Mary, John. L to R: Frances Black, Emily and Harry Woods, Lydia Bemmels, Lettie Cowman, Jessie McGregor.

Shanghai Bible School students and faculty. Missionaries (2nd Row L to R): Ina and Harry Shreve, Eugene Erny, Orville French – circa 1940

China Great Village Campaign, 1935. Missionary leader: Rolland Rice

OMS Shanghai Bible School evangelistic teams. Far L and R: Bud and Hazel Kilbourne, center R: Lettie Cowman

Peking women's Great Village Campaign team with Rosalind Rinker – 1931

Peking Great Village Campaign team with Uri Chandler and Rolland Rice – 1940

Lettie Cowman and Lydia Bemmels, Peking – Circa 1935

OMS Canton Bible School students with Lettie Cowman and Aileen French

OMS Peking Bible School graduates and missionaries (L to R): Rolland Rice, Will Shubert, Harry and Emily Woods, Aletta Jacobsz, Eunice Marais, Rosalind Rinker

Peking Great Village Campaign bands – 1939

India evangelistic team – circa 1945

OMS India Bible School evangelistic team. Wesley Duewel, with hat, center

OMS Allahabad Bible Institute, 1949. Missionaries: 2nd row (L to R): Meredith and Christine Helsby, Rev. and Mrs. Khanna, Esther and Eugene Erny, Walter and EuniceAnderson; 3rd row (L): Ed and Dorothy Bruerd, Esther Close, (center) Vera MacIlfatrick, (R) Evelyn Butler, Fred Buys, Bill McIlfatrick

Chapter 19

THE MEXICO CRUSADE

In November of 1941, a matter of weeks before the attack on Pearl Harbor, an invitation arrived inviting Lettie to attend the world's Sunday School Convention in Mexico City. Mrs. Cowman was now 71. Ordinarily the Spanish translator of *Streams*, Antonio Serrano, would have been the logical choice to represent OMS at such a conference, but at the time he was pastoring two churches and felt he could not attend. Still, Lettie thought it important that an OMS representative be there. Thus, under a kind of divine compulsion, she, accompanied by Lydia Bemels, her companion and nurse, journeyed to Mexico.

Strangely, Lettie felt led to stay on in Mexico three weeks after the convention had closed as she still did not know God's purpose in bringing her here. Then invitations came to speak, first at Mexico City's large Methodist church and another from the Union Seminary. Her interpreter was Dr. Fredrick J. Huegel, the well-known author of *Bone of His Bone*, a book so powerful that Lettie had ordered a copy for every OMS missionary. Huegel was fluent in Spanish and knew the meaning of being filled with the Spirit. As he interprets, he seems to be no less than the divine voice of God with a message for every believer in Mexico.

After the message, a young lady approached and pressed a peso, the equivalent of 21 cents, in Lettie's hand. In halting English she said, "This is to begin a new crusade in Mexico." "What is that among so many?" Lettie thought. Then she seemed to hear the Lord say, "Give ye them to eat."

As she prepared for her second and last scheduled meeting, she thought to herself, "If ever God must do something new in Mexico, now is the time." Sixty students gathered that evening. Again she told how the vision came to Charles Cowman. They seemed to see those first young evangelists take the Gospel to Japan's 10,400,000 homes. Then she described Charles' terrible Gethsemane years. The students now join in prayer for crusades in every nation. They join the Cowman's "army" as she launches Gospel distribution in 26 nations. If God through Charles E. Cowman in five years of The Great Village Campaign reached the homes of Japan, then God could use these volunteers to do the same in the great nation "south of the border."

In the seminary audience that night is Alexandro Guzman, a Salvation Army captain and dynamic preacher. While he was yet a Catholic, a Gospel portion was given him. He read it secretly and was converted. God called him to Christian service. He rose, left all and followed. For ten years he had been God's fire brand, a man of great spiritual power and influence.

The next day Lettie's telephone rings. It is Dr. Huegel. "May Captain Guzman and I see you in the prayer room of the Gante Methodist Church at 10:30 this morning?" he asks. When they meet Dr. Huegel says, "Captain Guzman and I spent last night in prayer. Mrs. Cowman, God has given us a vision for an Every Creature Crusade for all of Mexico. Just like you and Charles, He has called us to put God's Word in every home."

Mrs. Cowman is quiet a moment. Then she asks, "Do you know what a crusade costs? It costs great sums of money but more than that it cost the life of my precious companion. That is why I am alone. You should not begin unless you are ready to go to the depths." The men's faces shone as they replied, "We have faced that. We are ready to go to the depths." A great tide of joy swept over Lettie. Then she said, "You should know I have little more than a widow's two empty hands. But I promise you that I will give you for the Scriptures whatever He puts in these hands."

In the stillness of the prayer room, God spoke. "For this purpose," He said, "I have brought you here." Much of the morning they spent on their knees under the overshadowing presence of the Almighty. With Mary, she said, "Behold the handmaid of the Lord. Be it unto me according to thy word." This was to be Lettie's sunset ministry. Now her heart is full with unspeakable joy. She accompanies Dr. Huegel and Captain Guzman to the Bible Society. They place an order for 100,000 Gospels. The bill is to be mailed to her.

Prayer groups are formed and crusaders recruited from various churches and trained in personal evangelism. Large maps are purchased to chart the progress of the campaign. Assured that everything is in order to launch the Mexico Every Creature Crusade, Mrs. Cowman returned to Los Angeles. As everyone knows bills always travel fastest. The one for the first 100,000 Gospels for Mexico was no exception, $878.05. It arrived so soon. But why the five cents, she wondered.

Back in the OMS office Monday morning, Lettie hands Miss Frances Black, the mission treasurer, the $15 received in Mexico. "Please add up all that has come in," she asked. In a few moments, Frances returned with an adding machine tape. "Your total is exactly $878.05." Now Lettie understands the five cents, an odd amount. How like her Heavenly Father. He knows what we need and can be trusted to supply the exact amount, even to the last five cents. The church leaders in Mexico agree that the campaign will be called a National Campaign.

Mrs. Cowman always loved to read the reports of the Gospel campaigns. The first day the Mexican crusaders placed scriptures in 400 homes. They returned rejoicing. Christians they encounter are overjoyed. "We ought to be doing this," they say. Some ask for Bibles. Bible Society colporteurs now want to join the effort. They begin selling Bibles and Scripture portions as never before. This was another token of God's blessing.

Not long after, Mrs. Cowman received a letter from Dr. Huegel. "God is blessing the crusade beyond anything we ever dreamed," he says. "I never saw churches so moved. They are calling crusade leaders faster than we can respond. This crusade could become the greatest evangelistic effort in the history of Mexico." A large truck is purchased, one that will not only carry 10,000 Gospels and a supply of food but also provide sleeping room for the crusaders.

From week to week the campaign seems to gather momentum. After Captain Guzman holds meetings in a large church in Mexico City, 200 persons dedicate themselves to join the work. The young crusaders boldly debate with priests. The Protestant church authorities seem to be given special power and special wisdom. The doctrines of purgatory, indulgences, meritorious pilgrimages, and worship of the saints collapse like a house of cards. People are beginning to understand that it is faith in Christ alone which takes away the sins of the world.

"Now," Dr. Huegel reports, "the crusade is spreading over Mexico City like wildfire. More and more Gospels will be needed." The 110 churches of the Mexico Presbyterian Synod join the campaign, and they will need 25,000 Gospels a month. Reports of healing come, one an unusual miracle. Rather than oppose the campaign, the Roman Catholics begin an exact duplication of the National Crusade. It is reported that they are printing 5,000,000 copies of the four Gospels. The first edition is out. Evangelical leaders are rejoicing in what they consider the greatest victory in the history of Mexican Protestantism. Previously Catholics had destroyed Gospels and the Bible has been a prohibited book. Captain Guzman, hearing that Catholics are distributing Scriptures, remarks, "You can't put out a fire with gasoline."

Mrs. Cowman later learned that Captain Guzman and a companion had gone to a small town near Mexico City. As they entered the plaza, they saw two men lying dead on the ground, victims of Catholic reprisals. Soberly contemplating the corpses of their fellow crusaders, Guzman turned to his companion and said, "How do you feel?" "I don't feel very good," was the reply. "Neither do I," he admitted, "but here's what we'll do. You start distributing on this side of town and I'll begin on the other side. Then we'll meet in the plaza or we will meet in heaven."

Word came of another crusade's martyr in the little town of Cinco Serores, Actipan. The young man was stabbed to death while preaching and distributing Gospels. His Indian comrades built a rough board box. His body was laid in the simple coffin and flowers piled high around it. Lettie's eyes blurred as she read the report. Through the mist she sees Charles' face. Charles was a crusade casualty. Now Mexico has three martyrs in the crusade. They are rejoicing in heaven. Mexico's Acts of the Apostles is being written. These heroic crusaders are finding the cross of Calvary is the doorway to resurrection. From Mexico's church one day these heroes shall deathless rise and march from their graves. Another statistic: number wounded is ten.

Now crusaders are swinging down along the states which border Guatemala and Oaxaca. They travel mountain regions where proper roads are not yet constructed. On one trip the Ford and trailer crossed rivers 17 times. Since in areas the roads are blocked by huge boulders and landslides, some of the crusaders carry dynamite to blast their way through.

At this point over 1,400,000 Gospels have been distributed. Presses cannot keep up with the demand. As the crusade gathers momentum, attracting larger and larger numbers, a question is raised: "Who is to get the credit for this great evangelistic effort?" Mrs. Cowman writes to Dr. Huegel, "How little I care for the earth's glory, my brother. I am not anxious that The Oriental Missionary Society be known in the crusade. Many years ago God stripped me of such things. It is sweet to be just hidden away with Him. It may be that some time in the autumn Miss Bemels and I can slip down to Mexico for a little quiet retreat and prayer together. I do not wish to be seen in the crusade. God is raising up precious Mexican workers. How I thank Him for this."

Chapter 20

THE AFTER YEARS

The years and events following the close of World War II combined to create a time of unprecedented opportunity and fervency for the cause of world missions. With the conclusion of the world's most terrible war and the atomic bombs on Hiroshima and Nagasaki, the popular notion promoted by President Wilson after World War I—that the world had seen the "the war to end all wars"—was laid to rest. There was no truth in the claim that the flowering of civilizations, science, industry, culture, and education would indeed bring peace on earth and goodwill towards men. The ancient hope that "the darkness shall turn to dawning and dawning to noonday bright" would likely not happen in our time, during the lifetime of this generation.

Trampling forever on this sanguine hope came an evil so gigantic, so massive, so heinous that instead of fostering heaven on earth, the world had now to deal with atomic and hydrogen bombs in the hands of butchers and sadistic hoards who aspired to slaughter their fellow man as illustrated by horrors of the holocaust and the rape of Nanking. All this promised a great deal more hell then heaven on earth.

Even Karl Barth, the morning star of the new theology, neo-orthodoxy, was convincing theologians of the necessity of reviving the Biblical doctrine of sin and human depravity and the need for repentance.

Millions of our young men, veterans and survivors of the dark war that brought the fall of the Axis power in Europe and Asia, had seen cities leveled and displaced millions desperate for food, medical and social services. If ever in human history man needed to recover a clear, realistic view of human nature and the depravity of humankind, it was now. And for Christians this was the time for a Gospel, offering food and charity but more importantly a Gospel of salvation for the millions of earth seeking to climb from the hellish ruins of two wars to the promise of new life in Christ.

Now, by common consent, the dogmas of the liberalism of the early 20th century should be radically amended or laid to rest. The depravity of man and an unblinking declaration of the utter hopelessness of our race apart from the plain and simple confession of sin should be embraced. Jesus Christ was, after all, not merely a gentle example of charity but the bleeding Lamb of God whose sacrifice on the cross provides man's only hope for salvation.

Billy Graham burst upon the scene in 1949. Hundreds of thousands began attending his crusades in America's major cities. Evangelical organizations sprang up like flowers after a spring rain, many of them in southern California of all places. The Billy Graham Evangelistic Association, Youth for Christ, Campus Crusade, Inter-Varsity, Young Life, the charismatic movement, and a plethora of new evangelical churches followed. In time this vision was extended to foreign countries through Youth For Christ, Youth With a Mission, Operation Mobilization, and renewed denominational focus on foreign missions.

OMS leaders and particularly their new president, Eugene Erny, formerly the mission's India field director, were impacted by a changing world view. He issued a call for a resumption of the Every Creature Crusade.

The second Every Creature Crusade was born in 1950 and continues to this day in the U.S. and Great Britain. Young men, mostly from Christian colleges, volunteered to give two and one-half years of their lives for evangelizing Japan, Taiwan, India and Latin America. Of the 30 some new crusaders from the U.S. and Great Britain, all but a few became career missionaries, pastors or evangelists. Their story will be told in the sequel to this book.

At age 80 Lettie Cowman reluctantly retired from the presidency of OMS and founded two new organizations, Cowman

Publications and World Gospel Crusades. Before long, however, poor health forced her to enter a nursing facility. Still God had one more vision for her. "God has told me," she informed her friends, "that I will pass from this life to meet Charles on Easter Sunday." So it was on Easter Sunday in 1960 she died in her sleep, her final warfare completed.

OTHER BOOKS BY ED ERNY

NO GUARANTEE BUT GOD
With Esther Erny
Brief biographies of the founders of The Oriental Missionary Society—converted Western Union executives, Charles Cowman and Ernest Kilbourne; Lettie Cowman, famed author of *Streams in the Desert*; Juji Nakada, dynamic Japanese pastor and evangelist.

THE STORY BEHIND *STREAMS IN THE DESERT*
The diary of Lettie Cowman for the year 1924, the final year of husband Charles' life, provides a window into the crucible of physical pain and emotional and spiritual turmoil from which emerged the classic devotional S*treams in the Desert*, destined to bless millions of sufferers.

THIS ONE THING
The biography of missionary leader and statesman, Eugene Erny, a member of the famed Asbury College Missionary team, who held evangelistic meetings throughout Asia in 1929-30. In China he met, courted and won the hand of a young missionary with The Oriental Missionary Society, Esther Helsby. Together they served in China and India until 1950 when Eugene was elected president of the mission, a position he held until 1969.

NOBIE
Nobie Pope Sivley with Ed Erny
A life begun in shame and remorse finds beautiful fulfillment as a young lady travels from West Texas to the remote waterways of Colombia, South America, to offer healing and the message of salvation.

UNDER THE SENTENCE OF DEATH
Valetta Steel with Ed Erny
The epic story of a young pastor, Henry Steel, who upon learning that he is dying of Hodgkin's disease, determines to give himself unreservedly to reaching the nations for Jesus Christ.

THRICE THROUGH THE VALLEY
Valetta Steel with Ed Erny
Valetta Steel, widow of Henry Steel (*Under the Sentence of Death*), tells of the series of tragedies which bereft her of her entire family, testing her faith to the limits of human endurance but also leading to unprecedented joy and fruitfulness.

YIPPEE IN MY SOUL
Margaret Bonnette with Ed Erny
An adventuresome young woman determined to live life to the hilt, Margaret was once engaged to three men at the same time! Later, with her beloved husband's death, she finds her dreams shattered and her life empty. Her search for God eventuates in a life-changing encounter and a date with destiny as God's healer in the remote mountains of Haiti.

HE GOES BEFORE THEM
Meredith and Christine Helsby with Ed Erny and Carroll Hunt Rader
A young missionary family caught in the cross currents of war find themselves Japanese prisoners of war in China during World War II. A moving story of God's miracle provision and quiet courage in the darkest days of the 20th century.

THE QUEST
A small booklet explaining in simple language what one needs to do to be a Christian. More than 100,000 copies in print, *The Quest* has also been translated into a number of foreign languages.

THE KEY GOOSE (And Other Lessons God Taught Me)
Mildred Rice with Ed Erny
Rich spiritual lessons seasoned with humor, gleaned from a lifetime of missionary service in China, Japan and Taiwan.

PRINCESS IN THE KINGDOM
Evelyn Bellande with Ed Erny
Born into a wealthy, aristocratic Haitian family, a young lady finds her dreams broken by a failed marriage and the dark diagnosis of cancer. In her despair, she discovers life and a mission to her own people.

"LORD, THIS IS NOT WHAT I HAD IN MIND
A series of essays detailing humorous and embarrassing episodes in the lives of missionary families.

WHAT NOW, LORD?
Margaret Brabon with Ed Erny
The story of Harold and Margaret Brabon who helped pioneer the work of The Oriental Missionary Society in Colombia, South America, during the dangerous years of "La Violencia." This is a true romance in which a beautiful, idealistic college coed, engaged to a ministerial student, improbably falls in love with a brilliant young chemist working for Henry Ford.

TO INDIA WITH LOVE
Esther Close with Ed Erny
The story of an intrepid missionary nurse in the villages of India.

LEGACIES OF FAITH, VOLUME I, II, III, IV, AND V
Daily devotional readings from great Christian authors, arranged by subject matter and indexed for the benefit of pastors, evangelists, teachers, and Christian workers.

UNDER HIS WINGS
Mary Payseur with Ed Erny
The story of a North Carolina farm girl called of God to serve as a missionary in China where she was imprisoned during World War II.

IN THE DAY OF TROUBLE
Flora Chen with Ed Erny
The courageous story of a Christian woman caught in the horrors of three wars.

MISSIONARY MAVERICK
Elmer Kilbourne with Ed Erny
The incredible and moving story of Elmer Kilbourne, grandson of OMS founder Ernest Kilbourne. Instrumental in helping found World Vision, he also established scores of institutions of mercy following the Korean War. In India he was greatly used of God in the building of more than 200 churches and the founding of Bible schools and seminaries.